Tax Answers
at a Glance

Tax Answers at a Glance
by Tim Smith FCA ATII, Iain Watson and Hugh Williams FCA

Published by
Law Pack Publishing Limited
10-16 Cole Street
London SE1 4YH
www.lawpack.co.uk

Printed in Great Britain

Important

For Laurie Leask

'In this world nothing can be said to be certain, except
death and taxes.'
Benjamin Franklin

Contents

What are 'fixed deductions'?

5. Pensioners and tax   43

What sort of state pension can you expect?
What pension schemes are available for the employed?
What pension schemes are available for the self-employed?
What are free-standing additional voluntary contributions?
How much can I pay into a pension scheme?
What are the new rules for carrying forward of pension contributions?
Is it worth paying into a pension scheme?
What are directors' pension schemes?
What are Stakeholder Pensions?

6. Self-employment and partnerships   47

Telling the taxman if you are going self-employed or starting a partnership
What is trading?
How do I calculate my taxable income from trading?
What expenses can you claim?
Can I pay myself?
What is the tax significance of holding trading stock?
What is the tax significance of work in progress?
What are debtors and what do I do about them?
What are creditors and what do I do about them?
What are capital allowances and agricultural and industrial buildings allowances?
Is there any special tax treatment for farmers?
Is there any special tax treatment for visiting sports stars and entertainers?
Is there any special tax treatment for Lloyd's insurance underwriters?
Is there any special tax treatment for subcontractors?
Is there any special tax treatment for owners of mineral rights and royalties?
How do I get tax relief for losses in my business?
Are there any special rules about claiming farm losses?
How many years of farm losses can one utilise before having
    to carry forward those losses?
What is Class 4 National Insurance?
What is a partnership?
Do you need to have a partnership deed?
What are limited liability partnerships?
What happens if partners change?
How are partnerships taxed?
How long do I have to keep my accounting records?

How might the Inland Revenue inquire into my tax affairs?

11. Trusts and estates 81

12. Corporation Tax 85

13. Non-residence, working overseas, etc.   93

14. Inheritance Tax   99

15. VAT 103

What is VAT?
What records do I need to keep if my business is VAT-registered?
How do I complete my VAT Return?

16. Stamp Duty 107

What is Stamp Duty?
When and how is Stamp Duty paid?

17. Other tax issues 109

Tax planning 'do's'
Tax planning 'don'ts'
Tax saving tips
Notable tax dates
What is the difference between tax 'avoidance' and tax 'evasion'?
How should I deal with the tax office?
Should I use an accountant?
How should I handle tax investigations?
How do I appeal against a tax demand if I think it is too high?

Postscript 121

Appendices 123

Glossary 145

Index 153

Introduction

There are many books on tax, for both the professional and lay reader, but my impression is that most of them seem to look rather heavy, even if they aren't. As a practising accountant I know only too well how clients will phone in with questions (perhaps quite simple questions) and that all they want is a simple answer. If our clients are asking that question then there must be a lot of taxpayers who don't use the services of a professional accountant and who have similar questions that they would like answered.

Accordingly this book is written almost in the style of a catechism. It is meant to home in on the questions, giving answers at a glance, rather than giving all the background information which, to be realistic, most taxpayers don't want or need.

The title 'Tax Answers at a Glance' came when I was talking about the concept to the London cabbie who was driving me away from Law Pack after they had commissioned me to write this book. 'Yeah, I can see that that would be a very useful book – one that gives tax answers at a glance'. So, to that unnamed London taxi driver, I raise my hat in gratitude for giving us the title for this book.

I also must thank my fellow authors Tim Smith and Iain Watson, as well as Jacky O'Donnell who typed the script and Claire Earnshaw who reviewed it.

Our aim is for this book to be published on an annual basis and so, with these regular updates, there are bound to be more questions that readers would like us to answer than we have included in this first edition. We would welcome contributions from our readership because their feedback will enable the next edition to be a further improvement on what we hope is already a sensible way of providing 'Tax Answers at a Glance'. If you have any comments or questions please call us on 01752 334950.

Hugh Williams
H .M. Williams, Chartered Accountants
Plymouth

Chapter 1

Tax in general

What are the different taxes that we have to pay?

Between us (private individuals and businesses, etc.), we pay the following taxes:

- Income Tax
- National Insurance
- Value Added Tax
- Capital Gains Tax
- Inheritance Tax
- Stamp Duty
- Corporation Tax
- Petroleum Revenue Tax
- Fuel Duties
- Tobacco Duties
- Spirit Duties
- Wine Duties
- Beer and Cider Duties
- Betting and Gaming Duties
- Air Passenger Duties
- Insurance Premium Tax
- Landfill Tax
- Climate Change Levy
- Customs Duties and Levies
- Vehicle Excise Duties
- Oil Royalties
- Business Rates
- Council Tax

It's quite a list, isn't it? A summary of the actual tax rates and allowances is provided at Appendix 1.

How much does the Government raise in tax and what does it spend it on?

The Government expects to have raised the following in tax in 2001/02:

	£bn	Selected percentages	Estimated sum paid by each of us to the Government £	
Income Tax	107	28%	2,140	
Corporation Tax	32	8%		
Petroleum Revenue Tax	2			
Capital Gains Tax	3		60	
Inheritance Tax	2		40	
Stamp Duty	8		160	
Total Inland Revenue	154	41%		
Value Added Tax	59	15%	1,180	
Fuel Duties	23	6%	460	
Tobacco Duties	7	2%	140	
Spirit Duties	2		40	
Wine Duties	2		40	
Beer and Cider Duties	3		60	
Betting and Gaming Duties	1		20	
Air Passenger Duty	1		20	
Insurance Premium Tax	2		40	
Landfill Tax	1			
Climate Change Levy	N/A			
Customs Duties and Levies	2			
Total Customs and Excise	103	27%		
Vehicle Excise Duties	4	1%	80	
Oil Royalties	1			
Business Rates	17	4%		
National Insurance	60	16%	600	
Council Tax	14	4%	280	
Other taxes	9			
Total Other Receipts	105	27%		
Interest and adjustments	21	5%		
Total Receipts	383	100%	**£7,660**	per head in 2001/02

On average each of us, adults and children,
pays the Government   **£5,360**   per year

               or   **£14.68**   per day

The Government is not planning to spend all of this, only £366 billion, giving themselves a £17 billion surplus.

On the previous page we have seen how the Government intends to spend £366 billion. The Government intends to spend this money roughly as follows:

	%	£bn approx.	This means spending the money per head as follows:
Health Service	34	125	2,500
Defence, Trade and Industry	24	87	1,757
Education	22	81	1,610
Transport and Housing	13	48	952
Law and Order	7	26	512
	100	366	£7,331

When are tax rates changed?

Recent governments have changed the method of deciding when tax rates should be changed (in other words, they have hopped about a bit) but, in principle, the announcements of the tax rates are given in the Budget statement and associated documentation which the Chancellor of the Exchequer makes usually in the third week of March each year. Those rates and allowances, etc. come into force on 6 April immediately following.

When it comes to National Insurance, these changes are announced as part of the Chancellor's pre-Budget report in November and these allowances give the Inland Revenue the chance to be prepared for the changes some months later.

However, Gordon Brown has begun to announce changes for future years (i.e. beyond the immediately succeeding year) in his Budget and so, to a certain extent, tax advisers have known a few tax rates for a considerable period in advance.

What is the Income Tax year?

The Income Tax year runs from 6 April in one year to 5 April in the next. One of the authors of this book has spent a considerable amount of time badgering the Inland Revenue, Chancellors and Treasury officials to change this cumbersome system by using a more sensible date. All other taxes end their financial years on 31 March and it would make sense for the Government to move the Income Tax year by a few days so that all tax year ends are coterminous.

The reason the tax year ends on 5 April is not a very logical one, and so, at the back of this book we include a short postscript on why we should move to a more sensible date.

In the old days, and we are talking hundreds of years ago, the Income Tax year began on 25 March (the Feast of the Annunciation or Lady Day).

Up to 1752 there were two European calendars operating using different days. Britain used the Julian Calendar, devised at the time of Julius Caesar, while the rest of the Continent (pretty well all the rest) used the Gregorian Calendar (introduced by Pope Gregory the Great) which meant that by the time we had reached 1752, the Continent was 11 days ahead of us. In that year the two calendars merged and Britain 'lost' 11 days. The Treasury said that they could not afford to lose 11 days and added 11 days on to the Income Tax year end. This meant that the Income Tax year in 1753 ended on 4 April.

In 1800 our Treasury, for some reason, thought that there was a leap year. The formula for leap years is that they are years which can be divided by four and, when there is a centenary year, when they can be divided by 400. 1800 could not be divided by 400 to give a whole number result and so it was not a leap year – our Treasury thought otherwise. So the Treasury added an extra day to the Income Tax year at that stage resulting in a tax year end of 5 April.

We said at the start of this answer that the answer wouldn't be a good one. We hope you agree with us that it is high time that this anachronism was changed.

What are business rates and Council Tax, and how is that money spent?

Business rates are the rates paid by businesses to central government via their local councils. They are like a tax and they don't go towards local services, except as part of government's handout to local authorities. They are assessed on the area of space occupied by businesses.

Council Tax is collected by local councils and goes towards the following local services:

- Planning and economic development
- Recreation and tourism
- Environmental health
- Refuse collection
- Education
- Social services
- Police
- Fire

Council Tax is assessed on the market value of domestic properties which are graded in bands from A to H. There is a 24 per cent discount where only one person lives in a property.

What is the Inland Revenue and what is The Treasury?

The Inland Revenue is the government department that is responsible for collecting most of the nation's direct taxes. Customs & Excise collect VAT and custom duties and other indirect taxes.

The Inland Revenue advises the Treasury on direct tax matters generally, but it is the Treasury, controlled by the government in power at the time that decides how much tax it wants to raise from taxpayers. It then works with the Inland Revenue to devise a system that enables that money to be collected. Customs & Excise do the same with indirect taxes.

Within the Inland Revenue there are Inspectors of Taxes who check that the correct amount of tax is being paid by individuals, trusts and companies. There are also the Collectors of Taxes who make sure that the money is collected.

Chapter 2

Income Tax

What is Income Tax and what do we pay it on?

It may sound strange but Income Tax is actually a temporary annual tax that the Government decides to keep going by means of an annual Finance Bill. It was introduced in 1799 as a means of financing the Napoleonic Wars, but even though those wars are well past, Income Tax seems still to be with us.

Income Tax is divided into different schedules and, within some of those schedules, different sub-divisions or 'cases'.

Taking the schedules, we have:

Schedule A – covers income from land, buildings, rents, leases, etc.

Schedule B – abolished

Schedule C – abolished

Schedule D – has been divided into:
- Case I – taxes income from trades;
- Case II – taxes income from professions or vocations;
- Case III – covers the tax on gross interest and other annual payments;
- Cases IV and V (which are always taken together) – tax overseas income from certain investments, etc.;
- Case VI – taxes miscellaneous profits, etc. not falling within any of the other cases.

Schedule E – taxes wages and salaries from employments and is divided into:
- Case 1 where the employee is resident in the UK and the work is done here;
- Case 2 where the work is done here by a non-resident;
- Case 3 where the work is done wholly abroad by a UK resident whose salary is remitted here.

Schedule F – taxes dividends, etc. paid by companies.

You may be excused for thinking that none of the above sounds either interesting or relevant. The authors hasten to agree and the (so-called) 'schedular system' has been subject to plans for abolition.

It might be more relevant if we now look at what income is not taxed (i.e. what is tax-free):

- Income from PEPs, TESSAs and ISAs
- Job Finders Grant
- Compensation for receiving mis-sold personal pensions

- Casual gambling profits
- Premium Bond winnings
- Lottery prizes
- Interest on certain holdings of National Savings Certificates
- Bonuses paid at the end of Save As You Earn contracts
- Maturity bonuses on: British Saving Bonds, National Development Bonds and Defence Bonds
- Interest on Post-War Credits
- Wedding and certain other presents from your employer
- Certain retirement gratuities and redundancy monies paid by your employer
- Certain allowances paid under the Job Release Scheme
- Additional pensions in relation to gallantry awards
- Your first £70 of interest each year from National Savings Bank Ordinary Deposits
- The capital part of a purchased life annuity
- Certain payments for additional service in the armed forces
- Disability pensions
- German compensation payments
- Housing grants paid by local authorities
- War Widows Pensions
- Scholarship or educational grants
- Certain Social Security benefits including:
  - Sickness Benefit, but not Statutory Sick Pay
  - Maternity Allowance, but not Statutory Maternity Pay
  - Attendance Allowance
  - Child Benefit
  - Mobility Allowance
  - Payments of Income Support, Family Credit or Housing Benefit and short-term Incapacity Benefit

You can be pretty certain that everything else of a revenue nature is going to be taxable.

What is the annual Income Tax Return?

This is a form issued each year to about nine million taxpayers, the purpose of which is for them to list their income and, if they wish to do it themselves, calculate the overall tax due and the dates by which it should be paid.

How do I know if I have to fill out a Tax Return and how do I get hold of one?

You will have to complete a tax return if you:

- are self-employed;
- are in partnership;
- are in receipt of income from land and property;
- are in receipt of any taxable benefits in kind from your employer;
- are a director;
- receive taxable capital gains;
- are sent one (if the Inland Revenue issues a Tax Return, it *has* to be completed by the taxpayer).

If you are in any doubt, you should go to your local Tax Office, advise them of your circumstances, and get them to confirm whether you should fill out a Tax Return.

If you need to get hold of a Tax Return then you should contact the local Tax Office and ask them to send you one (better still visit the offices).

A checklist of what to keep for your Tax Return is provided at Appendix 2.

What are Working Families and Disabled Persons Tax Credits?

These are allowances payable under the Working Families Tax Credit scheme which were introduced in April 2000.

From that date, tax credits for employees will be paid through the PAYE system with their wages. This system replaces family credit and disability working allowance.

If you think you are entitled to either of these allowances then you should contact Social Security who, by liaising with the Inland Revenue, will ensure that you are paid these sums through your pay.

What is Children's Tax Credit?

Children's Tax Credit reduces the Income Tax you need to pay if you have a child under 16 living with you. It is worth up to £520 per year and is given through your tax code.

The qualifying conditions are:

- you have a child who lives with you for at least part of the tax year;
- the child is aged under 16;

- the child is your own (including a step-child or adopted child) or a child you look after at your expense.

The tax is not paid in full if a claimant is a higher rate taxpayer. It will be withdrawn at the rate of £1 for each £15 of income taxed at the higher rate. If one of a couple is a higher rate taxpayer, it must be this person that claims so that the restriction can be applied.

For couples where neither is a higher rate taxpayer, the tax credit may be claimed by either partner or shared between them.

How do I work out how much tax I have to pay and when to pay it?

If you have to complete a Tax Return, included in the package will be a tax calculation guide for you to follow.

It is not within the scope of this book to guide you through that (the Inland Revenue form does it pretty well for you), but the main thing to bear in mind is that if you get your tax return submitted by 30 September each year, the Inland Revenue will work out for you how much tax you have to pay and when you have to pay it.

In principle you make two payments a year. On 31 January each year you will pay the balance of the previous year's tax still owing plus one half of the previous year's tax liability as a payment on account for the following year.

On 31 July each year you will pay the second half of last year's tax liability. On 31 January following, you will find yourself paying any balance of tax that is due plus one half of next year's tax liability based on this year's total tax bill and so on.

If this all sounds very confusing, don't worry, it is! The Government introduced self-assessment in 1997 with the intention that tax recording and calculations should be so simple that anybody could do it. If you ask most professional accountants nowadays they would say that the current tax rules are so complicated they would find it very difficult to work out your tax liability if they didn't have the services of a computer.

What self-assessment has done is remove a lot of the work that was previously done in Tax Offices and dump it either on the taxpayer's own desk or, if the taxpayer is prepared to pay for it, in the offices of professional accountants, who now do the work that the Inspectors of Taxes formerly did.

In other words, self-assessment does not mean a simple calculation. It means 'It is up to you mate and don't blame us if we, the Inland Revenue, have made it difficult!'

What if my tax payments are late?

An interest charge is:

- automatic on late paid Income Tax, Class 4 National Insurance contributions and Capital Gains Tax;
- added to existing liabilities and treated as tax due and payable.

A surcharge applies to all amounts due on 31 January following the end of the tax year and not paid by 28 February. This is 5 per cent of the amount unpaid more than 28 days after the due date with a further 5 per cent of the amount unpaid more than six months after the due date

However, the taxpayer may appeal against a surcharge if he has a reasonable excuse.

What happens if I fail to complete a Tax Return on time?

If you are preparing a Tax Return there is an automatic fixed £100 penalty (or 100 per cent of the tax if less) if your Tax Return is not filed by the statutory filing date, 31 January in the following year. There is a further fixed £100 penalty if the return is not filed six months after the statutory filing date, i.e. following 31 July.

In addition, there are daily penalties (maximum £60 per day) imposed by Revenue determination following direction by tax commissioners.

Tax-geared penalties may also be imposed where the tax is paid more than one month late.

What can I set against my tax bill?

There is no quick answer to this question because there is a whole range of deductions, allowances, reliefs and expenses that taxpayers can claim. In principle, everybody is entitled to a personal allowance (and there is a number of different types of personal allowance, including increased allowances for the elderly), but apart from that it all depends on your circumstances. The sorts of relief that we, as accountants, see our clients claiming and that we can claim on their behalf are as follows:

- relief for losses in a business;
- relief for personal pension contributions;
- relief for Gift Aid payments;
- relief for investments made under either the Venture Capital Trust or Enterprise Investment Schemes;
- blind person's allowance;
- relief for interest borrowed for certain purposes;

- business expenses;
- certain allowances against capital gains.

We do advise you to read the Inland Revenue guidance notes that come with your Tax Return carefully to be sure that you are claiming all of your relief, but it simply isn't possible to list them all in the space of a book that gives you quick and easy to comprehend answers.

What is the difference between earned and unearned income?

About 25 years ago it was better to be in receipt of earned income than unearned income because unearned income attracted investment income surcharge and there was a special earned income relief.

Nowadays it is better to be in receipt of unearned income because earned income (salaries, wages, benefits, etc.) is not only taxable but is also subject to National Insurance contributions.

The distinction between the two is not a key one nowadays, but one of the more obvious distinctions arises in the case of a director shareholder. If he or she is paid a salary then both the company and the director must pay National Insurance contributions on that salary. The payment of £1,000 as earnings may result in about one third of that figure going to the Government. If that same person is paid a dividend out of taxed profits, no further tax will be due to the Government although, in due course, there may be tax payable by the director when it comes to completing the personal Tax Return.

Personal reliefs and allowances

The rates of the various personal reliefs and allowances for 2001/2002 are as follows:

		£
Personal		4,535
Children's Tax Credit		*5,200
Age		
• personal	(age 65–74)	5,990
• married couple's	(age 65–74) and born before 6 April 1935	*5,365
• personal	(age 75 and over)	6,260
• married couple's	(age 75 and over) and born before 6 April 1935	*5,435
Relief for blind person		1,450

*indicates allowances where tax relief is restricted to 10%

What tax relief can I claim against my payments of interest?

Opportunities to claim tax relief on payments of interest on loans are limited and are now restricted to the following:

- the purchase of life annuities if you are aged 65 or over;
- buying a share in a partnership or contributing capital to a partnership if you are a partner;
- buying a share in a close company (see page 88) or lending capital to it;
- buying plant and machinery for use in a job or partnership.

The interest paid (and not the capital) is deducted from your total income in the year of payment.

Can I get tax relief on my mortgage?

Unfortunately, since 5 April 2000, tax relief on mortgage interest payments has been withdrawn; this applies to both interest paid under MIRAS (mortgage interest relief at source) or otherwise.

Is there a right time to get married for Income Tax purposes?

The married couple's allowance was withdrawn on 6 April 2000, except for those couples where either the husband or wife was aged 65 or more at 5 April 2000.

However, if you get married and you were over 65 on 5 April 2000 or your spouse was, you can claim 1/12th of the allowance for each month of the Tax Year concerned, starting with the month of marriage. So there is no 'best time' to get married for Income Tax purposes.

Is there a right time to get divorced or separate for Income Tax purposes?

For those who are still able to claim the married couple's allowance, this is not reduced in the year when couples separate or in the year of death of either spouse. However, with being so restricted as to its use, this matter is now of little consequence to parties when they divorce or separate.

What happens to someone's Income Tax affairs when they die?

When someone dies, they are entitled to their normal full year's worth of allowances. A Tax Return will need to be completed for the last period of life up to date of death and the tax worked out accordingly.

Income arising after death is treated as the income of the estate and becomes the responsibility of the trustees or executors. When the estate is distributed, both the capital and the income that has arisen since the date of death will be distributed according to the Will to the various beneficiaries and tax will be deducted from any income that has been received at the appropriate rate.

If you as a beneficiary are in receipt of income that has been credited to a deceased person's estate, then you will receive that income net of the appropriate rate tax and while you may have to pay higher rate tax on the income, there is also a chance that you might be able to claim some back or for there to be no adjustment at all.

What should one do about the income of children and Income Tax?

Children, from the moment they are born, are entitled to a personal allowance and if they are in receipt of income, apart from dividends, they are almost certainly entitled to a repayment of tax. Accordingly, where children are in receipt of income from which tax has been deducted, it is potentially refundable. Get a tax claim form from the Tax Office (note it is called a tax claim and not a Tax Return, but it amounts to the same thing). When you have completed it and sent it in, the Inland Revenue will either send a cheque in favour of the child or make a refund of tax straight to that child's own bank or building society account.

What are the most sensible sorts of investment for children for tax purposes?

The simplest answer is that savings accounts with building societies or banks that are in the children's names should pay the children interest gross (i.e. without tax deducted).

It is still quite permissible for children to hold shares in companies, even though the tax credits on the dividends are not refundable.

If the children do not have any investments and if the parents have surplus after-tax income of their own which they give to their children, this is usually tax-free in the children's hands and, if the parents are particularly wealthy, is a very useful way of transferring income to them, so that the children can accumulate a sum that can then be invested. However, once the income from the source exceeds £100 p.a. it will be taxed in the hands of the parents. Where parents transfer their own shares to their children, if the children are under 18, the income arising on these shares will be regarded as belonging to the parents, so this does not save tax.

What are the new rules for charitable giving and Income Tax?

- The £250 minimum limit for Gift Aid donations has been abolished.

- The separate tax relief for payments made under a deed of covenant has been withdrawn.

- The Gift Aid certificate has been replaced by a simpler and more flexible Gift Aid declaration. If you turn to Appendix 6 you will see an example of this and how it works. However, remember this will only work if you have paid more tax than will be reclaimed by the charity. Otherwise the Inland Revenue will send you a bill for the difference.

- The £1,200-a-year ceiling for Payroll Giving has been abolished.

- There is a new and potentially generous tax relief for gifts of certain shares and securities to charity.

What do I do with deeds of covenant now that there are the new rules for charitable giving?

You do not have to get a Gift Aid declaration in respect of payments under a deed of covenant that was already in existence before 6 April 2000. The deed of covenant will stand in place of the Gift Aid declaration. However, any donations made outside the terms of the deed, or after the expiry of the deed, must be covered by a Gift Aid declaration. Likewise, payments made under a deed of covenant executed on or after 6 April 2000 must be covered by a Gift Aid declaration.

What is 'Payroll Giving'?

Employees can arrange a regular deduction from their pre-tax pay to go to a nominated charity, church or charitable association. The minimum donation is £1 per month or 25p per week, with no maximum.

The tax that would have been deducted under PAYE now goes to the charity instead of the Inland Revenue. Until 5 April 2003, the Inland Revenue will top up the donation by a further 10%. This means that a donation of £5 is worth £5.50 and actually costs the employee only £3.90.

Employers need to sign an administration contract with an authorised Payroll Giving Agency. They do make a small administration charge that is either deducted from the donation or can be paid separately by the employer (of the order of 4–5 per cent).

How do I reclaim overpaid tax?

If you are likely always to pay too much tax (through receiving no gross income, i.e. all your income suffers tax at source), the Inland Revenue will spot this and will no longer send you a form called a Tax Return, but a tax claim form instead. It amounts to the same thing but will probably be returnable to a Tax Office that deals solely with tax repayments.

If on the other hand you normally pay tax but in a certain year discover that you have overpaid, once your Tax Return has been submitted, and if you tick the appropriate box on that Tax Return, you can claim for the money to be refunded to you. If you leave the overpayment unrefunded it will go to reduce your future year's tax payments.

Chapter 3

National Insurance

What is National Insurance?

National Insurance contributions are an extra and important tax that has to be paid on certain sources of income. The contributions paid are, in principle, used to pay for an individual's following state benefits:

- State Retirement Pension
- Widows' Pension
- Widows' Payment
- Widowed Mothers' Allowance
- Maternity Allowance
- Incapacity Benefit
- Job Seekers' Allowance

What are the different classes of National Insurance?

There are four classes of National Insurance, and some have sub-divisions.

- **Class 1** – is paid by employers and employees on employees' earnings. Class 1A is paid on employees' benefits in kind. (See also 'What National Insurance is payable on employees' benefits?', page 40.)

- **Class 2** – is paid by the self-employed (but see also Class 4).

- **Class 3** – is a voluntary contribution which you can pay in order to protect your benefits, if you are not otherwise paying National Insurance contributions, e.g. this might arise because you have no earnings on which National Insurance is payable, but you still want to pay for a state pension.

- **Class 4** – is an additional National Insurance contribution paid by the self-employed whose earnings exceed a certain sum. Class 4 contributions do not provide any further benefits for the contributor.

You will not have to pay National Insurance contributions if you have retired or have passed normal retirement age (60 for a woman and 65 for a man). However, if you are still working beyond the age of 65, your employer still remains liable for its National Insurance contributions.

Who pays what?

National Insurance – the basic facts for 2001/2002

(a) Employees pay 10 per cent of their earnings between £4,524.00 p.a (£87 per week) and a top limit of £29,900 (£575 per week).

(b) Employers pay 11.9 per cent on their employees' earnings over £87 per week (£4,524 p.a.). There is no upper limit.

(c) Men over 65, women over 60 and children under 16 pay nothing. However, employers still have to pay up to 11.9 per cent on their earnings.

(d) The self-employed pay £2.00 per week when their profits are £3,955 or more.

(e) In addition, self-employed people with profits over £4,535 pay 7 per cent on all profits between £4,535 and £29,900 (i.e. maximum £1,775.55).

(f) Self-employed taxpayers with low earnings (less than £3,955) can elect to pay nothing – indeed they must do so or else they may find they have to pay extra contributions when the National Insurance Inspector comes along.

(g) If you do not come into any of the above categories (i.e. if you are going abroad) you can elect to pay £6.75 a week in order to maintain your contributions record.

(Note: Items (a), (b), and (c) are called Class 1; (d) and (e) are Class 2; (g) is Class 3 and (f) is Class 4.)

What do I get for my money?

Table 1 below gives you an indication of what the different classes of National Insurance contributions pay for:

Table 1

Type of Benefit	Class 1 (Employed)	Class 2 (Self-employed)	Class 3 (Voluntary)
Retirement Pension Basic	Yes	Yes	Yes
Retirement Pension Additional	Yes	No	No
Widows' Pension	Yes	Yes	Yes
Widows' Payment	Yes	Yes	Yes
Widowed Mothers' Allowance	Yes	Yes	Yes
Maternity Allowance	Yes	Yes	No
Incapacity Benefit	Yes	Yes	No
Job Seekers' Allowance	Yes	No	No

How are National Insurance contributions paid?

- **Class 1** contributions are paid on a weekly or monthly basis by the employer (secondary contributions). The employer deducts his employees' contributions (primary contributions) from their gross pay (along with Income Tax and other deductions) and pays that sum over, together with his own contributions, by the 19th of the following month.

- **Class 2** contributions are paid by monthly direct debit.

- **Class 3** contributions are paid by monthly direct debit.

- **Class 4** contributions are calculated along with the self-employed's Self Assessment Income Tax calculation and paid once or twice a year, with the Income Tax payments. (This applies to any Class 4 contribution.)

How do I find my National Insurance number?

If you don't know your National Insurance number write to the local Contributions Agency (whose address and telephone number you will find in the telephone book) and ask them to give you your National Insurance number, telling them your:

- full name
- maiden name
- date of birth
- date of marriage
- present address

What happens if I should be paying National Insurance contributions but fail to do so?

Make no mistake, this can be expensive if you start up either as an employer who fails to deduct tax and National Insurance contributions from your employees' wages, or you start in self-employment and fail to register with the Inland Revenue.

If as an employer you fail to pay over the correct National Insurance contributions for your employees by 19 April following the end of the Tax Year, not only will these have to be paid over, but in addition there will be interest due on the late payment and, in addition to that, there will be penalties for failing to make the payments on time.

If you are an employee whose employer is failing to deduct contributions from your pay and pay them over to the Inland Revenue, you cannot be held liable to make the payment yourself. It is the employer's responsibility. Our understanding of the law is that, since it is the employer's responsibility, there is no way in which the Inland Revenue can get you to pay the National Insurance contributions that should have been deducted from your gross pay nor should your benefits be affected, because the Revenue will collect the contributions from your employer.

In the case of the self-employed, it is fairly unusual nowadays to find someone not paying the correct Class 2 or Class 4 contributions. The reason is that the Inland Revenue is now responsible for National Insurance contributions. When a self-employed person wishes to register as such with the Inland Revenue, the forms are designed in such a way that the National Insurance obligations are dealt with at the same time. In other words, if you are self-employed and not paying Class 2 contributions, you will not be registered with the Inland Revenue at all. The problems could well be exacerbated because, if you are not paying Class 2 contributions, you are not paying income tax and Class 4 contributions either.

In other words we are hoping that the answer to this question is fairly academic. However, in the cases where Class 2 contributions are not being paid by self-employed people they face a 'double whammy'. Not only do they have to pay for all the past years' National Insurance contributions at the current year's rate (which up until 2000/01 was usually higher than the rate that applied in the years for which contributions should have been made, but weren't) but, in addition, only the last two years of contributions being paid at this late stage actually count towards State benefits, etc.

In short, if you are self-employed, don't fail to pay your National Insurance contributions.

Of course, if your earnings are below the exception threshold then you are not obliged to make the contributions but, to be sure that everything is in order, you do have to apply for an 'exception certificate' and this you can do by approaching the Inland Revenue.

In the case of Class 4 contributions not being paid, this calculation and payment forms part of the Income Tax calculation and payment and therefore, on the assumption that accounts have been submitted and the Tax Return approved by the Inland Revenue, they will very soon spot if you are not paying Class 4 contributions and put the matter right.

What should I do if I am worried that my National Insurance contributions are not up to date?

You should contact the National Insurance Contributions Office and find out exactly where you stand with regard to contributions you have made and benefits you are entitled to.

What is Class 4 National Insurance?

This is the extra National Insurance 'tax' that has to be paid by the self-employed when their earnings exceed a certain threshold. It is an additional tax, and tax is the right word because it actually buys no further benefits for the payer. It is calculated as part of the self-assessment tax and Class 4 National Insurance calculation and paid with Income Tax on the same dates as Income Tax.

What if I have overpaid National Insurance contributions?

There is an annual maximum contribution that someone who is both an employee and self-employed or has two jobs should pay and if they have paid more than that threshold, they can apply to the Inland Revenue to have the surplus refunded. The maximum figure for 2001/02 is 53 weeks at £48.80 or £2,586.40.

Chapter 4

Employment and Income Tax

What do I do if I employ somebody?

Taking somebody on can be one of the early big milestones in any business. What follows can also apply to private individuals who are employing people such as cooks, nannies, gardeners, etc. and so, while most of what follows relates to the things that a business person should do, private individuals should be aware that they may well be caught by the PAYE regulations that relate to employing people.

There is no easy answer to this very simple question. Having said this the only answer is that you have to obey the law but knowing what the law is is not always easy in itself.

If you take on somebody and you are paying them more than £87 a week, no matter what their age, you have to pay National Insurance contributions and the rate is 11.9 per cent. If this is the case then the first thing you should do is inform the Inland Revenue that you have taken somebody on and the second thing you should do is decide how you are going to handle the PAYE payment obligations. In our view the simplest way of meeting your obligations is to ask a professional accountant to look after the PAYE side of things for you. They will tell you how much to pay your employees net of tax and National Insurance and they will also send you the appropriate PAYE slip for making the monthly or quarterly payments to the Inland Revenue. They will also be able to help you with the annual return (P35) and with the benefit forms (P11Ds).

A second alternative is to buy a simple computer program and do the work in-house yourself. These are good, economically priced and well worth the investment in both software and stationery.

A third alternative is to use the manual forms the Inland Revenue send you. In our view these are not easy forms to follow and definitely a worse option than the first two suggestions above.

A fourth alternative is to go and buy a manual wages system from the local stationer. This would certainly be better than using the Inland Revenue forms but, in this computer centred age, we certainly recommend options 1 and 2.

However, it could be that you take on somebody who is earning less than £87 a week (so there is no National Insurance contribution for you to worry about) but, because they are being employed elsewhere, Income Tax should be deducted, perhaps even from the first pound you pay them. In other words when you take somebody on they may hand you a form (P45) which will give you all the details you need to set them up in the PAYE system and, even though you are paying them a small sum, that very form might direct you to deduct Income Tax.

Alternatively they may be coming to work for you and already have another job, which is going to continue, and under those circumstances a form P15 should be completed so that the Inland Revenue will send you a notice of coding which, again, might well direct you to deduct tax from all the wages that you are paying.

We said at the start that there is no easy answer to this and perhaps the best answer to give you is to go and discuss the matter with the Inland Revenue or with a professional accountant. Make no mistake. It is a complicated business and one that is very important to get right. Employers should not turn a blind eye to their obligations.

Is the person you are taking on an employee or self-employed?

As with the above question there is no easy answer to this. There have been many painful cases brought to light by a visiting Inland Revenue PAYE investigator. Employers who thought that all their employees were self-employed have discovered to their horror and great expense that they should have been deducting tax and National Insurance from the gross payments that they have been making to their staff.

Below you will find a list of questions that you should ask which will help you decide whether the person whose services you are using is self-employed or an employee.

As practising accountants we are of the opinion that, if somebody is 'employed' on a regular basis, but is regarded by both parties as self-employed (and the following questionnaire justifies this decision), a contract should be signed by both parties which can be shown to the Inland Revenue and which clearly establishes that the arrangement is one of self-employment.

Employed or self-employed? A questionnaire to help you decide

The Inland Revenue are keen to classify self-employed people as employees because this increases National Insurance contributions and Income Tax.

How can you tell if someone is an employee or is self-employed? Answering the following questions should help. Note: there are separate and new rules for workers in the construction industry; the following questions are not appropriate for such workers.

1. Is there a contract of service i.e. a contract of employment?
    A No answer indicates self-employment

2. Is there a contract for services i.e. a notice supplied by the person carrying out the work (A), indicating the nature of goods or services he or she will provide to B? (this need not be written)
    A Yes answer indicates self-employment

3. Is the person who does the work in business on his or her own account?
   A Yes answer indicates self-employment

4. If the person is in business on his or her own account has evidence been provided that this is indeed the case – e.g. copy accounts, the payment of Class 2 National Insurance contributions?
   A Yes answer indicates self-employment

5. Are the hours worked decided by the person doing the work?
   A Yes answer indicates self-employment

6. Are the days worked decided by the person doing the work?
   A Yes answer indicates self-employment

7. Does the person doing the work decide when to take his or her own holidays?
   A Yes answer indicates self-employment

8. Does the business proprietor supervise the work
   A No answer indicates self-employment

9. Is the person part and parcel of the business?
   A No answer indicates self-employment

10. Does the person supply tools and/or materials when he or she carries out the work?
    A Yes answer indicates self-employment

11. Does the person doing the work give the business an invoice for the work done?
    A Yes answer indicates self-employment

12. Does the business calculate how much to pay the person doing the work and give a payslip?
    A No answer indicates self-employment

13. Is self-employment the intention of both parties?
    A Yes answer indicates self-employment

14. Is the person bound by the customer care credo of the business?
    A No answer indicates self-employment

15. Is the person carrying out the work required to wear a uniform or dress tidily at the diktat of the business?
    A No answer indicates self-employment

16. Is the person carrying out the work provided with a car or transport by the business?
    A No answer indicates self-employment

17. In the event of sickness, does the business continue to pay the person while not at work?
A No answer indicates self-employment

18. Is the person carrying out the work at liberty to work for other businesses?
A Yes answer indicates self-employment

19. Is the person carrying out the work required to work in order to perform a specific task?
A Yes answer indicates self-employment

20. Does the business, on asking this person to carry out work for them, assume any responsibility or liability characteristic of an employment, such as employment protection, employees' liability, pension entitlements, etc.?
A No answer indicates self-employment

21. Is the person who does the work paid an agreed price per job?
A Yes answer indicates self-employment (i.e. they are not paid for the hours they work but for the work carried out)

22. Is the work carried out regularly?
A No answer indicates self-employment

23. Does the individual work for other people?
A Yes answer indicates self-employment

24. Does the person carrying out the work advertise?
A Yes answer indicates self-employment

25. Does the person carrying out the work have headed stationery?
A Yes answer indicates self-employment

26. Can the person send a substitute? If so, has this ever happened?
A Yes answer indicates self-employment

27. Do they have to rectify faulty workmanship in their own time and at their own expense?
A Yes answer indicates self-employment

Having addressed these questions you should now begin to know whether in reality the person under consideration is an employee or is self-employed. However, a definite answer can only be given by the courts.

What if I take on someone part-time or casually?

This is probably the most difficult employment question of all to answer. The typical accountant's answer is 'it all depends'. Our view is that if you read the three preceding questions you will get a pretty good idea of your obligations. If you take on someone casually on both an infrequent, irregular (possibly one-off) basis, the Inland Revenue is very unlikely to be concerned about the matter. There is a very well-known legal maxim 'de minimis non curat lex', which means 'the law is not concerned with trifles'. The authors think that the best advice we can give to the reader is to say 'Is this a trifle?'. If it is, and you can justify it as being such to a visiting inspector, then regard the person as being casual – a trifle. If the matter has obviously some regularity and (shall we say) meaty content – in other words not a trifle – then we suggest that you go and talk it through with the Inland Revenue or an accountant and take the action that arises from such an approach.

What is PAYE?

PAYE stands for Pay As You Earn. It represents a logical system whereby week by week or month by month, an employer deducts tax and National Insurance in such a way that, at the end of the income tax year, the right amount of tax and National Insurance has been deducted and handed over to the authorities. It works in the following way:

Let us say that you earn £15,000 a year and that your personal allowance is £3,000. Let us also suppose that the rate of tax that you are paying is 10 per cent (wouldn't that be nice?)

If you paid your tax just once a year you would take your pay –

- £15,000 less your tax free personal allowance £3,000
- Taxable pay £12,000
- Tax @ 10 per cent £1,200

The way PAYE works is to collect that £1,200 on a monthly basis and that works as follows:

The Inland Revenue issue tables that show the tax-free pay for each of the various PAYE codes for each week and for each month throughout the year. They also issue tax tables that tell you how much tax to deduct from somebody's pay for each of the weeks and months throughout the year. We won't go into the details here (your eyes may be glazing over already by now) but if we take the case of somebody with a tax allowance of £3,000 that would equate to a PAYE code of 300. During the year, at whatever payment date you were making a wages or salary payment you would look up the appropriate amount of free pay for somebody with a tax code of 300 at that moment. What you would find is that if you were paying somebody £15,000 a year each month you would pay them £1,250.

In addition to this you would be giving them £250 tax free pay (you would find this in Table A of the documentation you are given by the Inland Revenue) so that you apply the tax rate of 10 per cent (using Table B) to the £1,000 taxable pay. This means that you would deduct £100 from the pay each month and send that off to the Inland Revenue. At the end of the year you would have paid over £1,200.

However, you have to remember that, in addition to doing this tax calculation, you would also have to work out the National Insurance. It is quite a palaver and this is why we recommend elsewhere in the book that anybody having to cope with the rigours of PAYE and National Insurance should use a computer or get somebody else to do it for them.

A payslip showing how gross and net pay should be set out is given at Appendix 3.

What is a tax code and what is a notice of coding?

Reference to the above question will give some sort of answer to this; however anyone who is being paid through PAYE will be given a notice of coding. This is a document which is sent to them by the Inland Revenue explaining how the Inland Revenue calculate their tax code. A much simpler document, simply giving the tax code, will be handed to the employer so that they know which tax code to apply to the employee's pay.

In other words a simple answer is – a tax code is a number given to an individual which enables the employer to work out how much tax to deduct and a notice of coding is the piece of paper on which that number has been printed by the tax authorities.

What if you fail to operate PAYE properly?

This can be very nasty. An employer who fails to operate PAYE properly can find that, when they are found out (and they will be found out), they have to pay over not only the tax that should have been deducted, not only the National Insurance contributions that should have been deducted, not only the National Insurance contributions that they as an employer should have been paying, but also interest on the late payment if it was paid after 19 April following the end of the tax year and a penalty for not having done it properly in the first place.

Don't fail to operate PAYE properly.

What records does an employer have to keep?

It has often struck us as strange that there is no complete and all-embracing PAYE recording system that you can buy in a stationery shop. We ourselves have often considered devising such a system, to help employers fulfil their obligations, but, to date, this has not been achieved.

A proper system for keeping employees' records would consist of the following:

For each employee:

- A contract of employment
- Notices of PAYE coding
- A permanent record sheet which would record: employees' name, date of birth, National Insurance number, date of joining, date of pay rises, etc.

But in addition you would need to keep properly filed away the Inland Revenue's instructions for employers:

- Table A
- Table B
- National Insurance instructions for employers
- National Insurance tables
- Pension fund details
- ... etc. etc.

In other words, an employer certainly has a number of important obligations. Our view is that, if an employer is doing his job properly, he will want to keep his records properly, pay his people properly and keep within the law. In our experience it is businesses that behave like this which succeed and flourish.

What is the National Minimum Wage?

The minimum you need to know

You must pay workers aged over 22 at least £3.70 per hour (aged 18 to 21: £3.20). If you are providing accredited training for someone over 22, then you must pay at least £3.20. This applies to every single worker over 18. The minimum wage came into effect on 1 April 1999 and regular updates are available at the DTI website: www.dti.gov.uk/er/nmw. In October 2001, the minimum wage increases to £4.10 per hour and to £4.20 per hour in October 2002.

The Inland Revenue may ask you to prove that you are paying at least the National Minimum Wage. So you must keep records.

Failure to comply can result in a hefty fine (up to £5,000 for each offence).

For more information contact the DTI information line on 0845 8450 360.

What is Statutory Sick Pay and Statutory Maternity Pay?

This book is not trying to deal in depth with tax issues and the best way of finding the full answer to this particular question is to refer either to the leaflets which are handed out by the Inland Revenue each year, or refer to Law Pack's Employment Law Guide.

However the principle is that when someone is sick the Government expects the employer to pay that person sick pay (Statutory Sick Pay) and such payments as the employers make (up to the Statutory Sick Pay figure) can, in principle, be deducted from the National Insurance payments that are made at the end of each quarter. Statutory Sick Pay is by no means generous and most employers find themselves paying more than the Statutory Sick Pay. However the principle is that the employer makes the payment and the Government reimburses the payment (or some of it) to that employer.

In the case of Statutory Maternity Pay (and it too is a complicated subject), the same principle applies, namely that the employer pays their employees who are absent to have babies and the Government reimburses such payment through the PAYE system.

What tax deductible expenses can an employee claim?

If you are an employee, which business expenses are deductible for tax purposes and which are not?

Clothes
Normally allowed – Cost of replacing, cleaning and repairing protective clothing (e.g. overalls, boots) and functional clothing (e.g. uniform) necessary for your job and which you are required to provide. Cost of cleaning protective clothing or functional clothing provided by your employer, if cleaning facilities are not provided.

Not allowed – Ordinary clothes you wear for work (e.g. pin-stripe suit) which you could wear outside work – even if you never choose to.

Tools, etc.
Normally allowed – Cost of maintaining and repairing tools and instruments which you are required to provide. Cost of replacing tools and instruments.

Not allowed – Initial cost of tools and instruments but may be able to claim capital allowances.

Cost of working at home

Normally allowed – Proportion of lighting, heating, telephone, cleaning, insurance, proportion of rent, Council Tax and water rates if part of home used exclusively for business. But these expenses are allowed only if it is necessary that you carry out your duties at or from home (i.e. if it is an express or implied condition of your employment). Claiming Council Tax, water rates or ground rent may mean some Capital Gains Tax to pay if you sell your home – but unlikely.

Stationery, etc.

Normally allowed – Cost of reference books which are necessary for your job and which you are required to provide. Cost of stationery used strictly for your job.

Not allowed – Cost of books you feel you need to do your job properly, but which are not necessary for it. Subscriptions to journals to keep up with general news.

Interest

Normally allowed – Interest on loans to buy equipment (e.g. a personal computer) necessary for the job.

Not allowed – Interest on overdraft or credit card.

Travelling

Normally allowed – Expenses incurred strictly in the course of carrying out the job. Running costs of own car. Until 5 April 2002 you may claim the whole of cost if used wholly and necessarily in carrying out your job, proportion of cost if used privately as well. Company car, if you pay for running costs (e.g petrol, repairs, maintenance), claim proportion of cost for business mileage.

Not allowed – Travel to and from work. Cost of buying a car – but you may be able to claim a capital allowance.

Accompanying spouses

Normally allowed – Cost of husband or wife travelling with you if he or she has, and uses, practical qualification directly associated with trip. Often only a proportion of cost is allowed.

Hotels and meals

Normally allowed – If you keep up a permanent home, reasonable hotel and meal expenses when travelling in the course of your job.

Others

Normally allowed – Pension scheme contributions.

What is the Working Time Directive?

The Working Time Regulations came into force on 1 October 1998. Implementing a hefty chunk of the EU Social Chapter, they make big changes to the regulation of working hours, but have received remarkably little publicity.

The rules cover all workers, full-time and part-time, regardless of the size of firm for which they work and including domestic servants. They extend to quite a few who, for tax purposes, would be counted as self-employed, such as freelancers.

The regulations provide that –

(a)   workers do not work more than 48 hours a week

(b)   night workers do not work more than 8 hours a night and are offered regular health assessments

(c)   workers have a rest period of 11 consecutive hours between each working day

(d)   workers have an in-work rest break of 20 minutes when working more than 6 hours

(e)   workers have at least 4 weeks paid leave each year.

Only in the case of the 48 hour week, may individual workers choose to agree to ignore the regulations and work more than 48 hours. If they do, the agreement must be in writing and must allow the worker to bring the agreement to an end.

There are a number of other flexibilities and a lot of detailed definitions. If you would like to learn more you can obtain a free copy of the DTI Guide to Working Time Regulations, by calling 0845 6000 925.

What about holiday pay?

Holiday pay is not really a tax issue, but it can be answered under this section.

Holiday pay would normally be dealt with in a contract of employment and all employees should be issued with a contract of employment by the employer. However, whether holiday pay is paid under a contract or under any other arrangement, it forms part of gross pay and is treated exactly the same as any other pay.

What are the rules about directors and tax?

If you are a company director and your company pays you wages, salary, bonus or commission, you must apply the PAYE procedures.

The Income Tax aspect is calculated in exactly the same way as for an employee, but there is a very important difference in the calculation of the National Insurance contributions. If you are a director, at 6 April you need to use the 'annual earnings period' calculation and if you became a director during the year you must use the 'pro-rata annual earnings period'.

Further details of these methods are given on card 13 in the Inland Revenue Employers Pack and in manual CA44, *National Insurance for Company Directors.*

What if I provide benefits for my employees?

Any benefits provided for employees must, in the first instance, be regarded as taxable and liable to be reported to the Inland Revenue.

If your employee is remunerated at a rate of less than £8,500 per year including benefits, then there are simpler reporting requirements on form P9D. Also, not all of the benefits are taxable.

If your employee is remunerated at a rate of £8,500 or more, or is a company director (regardless of earnings) then full details must be reported on form P11D. Inland Revenue booklet 480 is an invaluable guide to the whole issue of expenses and benefits payments.

The time limit for submitting forms P9D and P11D to the Tax Office is 6 July following the Tax Year end. A P11D form is reproduced at Appendix 4, for reference.

The class 1A NIC liability on the employer for any benefits made available to employees is calculated using the P11D information.

What are the rules about providing motor cars for my employees?

The provision by an employer of a car or van, partly or wholly for private use by an employee, is the subject of a 'car scale charge'. The charge is based on the manufacturer's list price (up to £80,000) of the car, which includes VAT, delivery, extras supplied with the car and accessories costing more than £100 that are added later. The employee can make a contribution of up to £5,000 and this reduces the cost on which the charge is based.

- For those travelling less than 2,500 business miles per annum, the charge is 35 per cent of the list price.

- For those travelling 2,500–17,999 business miles per annum, the charge is 25 per cent of the list price.

- For those travelling 18,000 business miles and over, the charge is 15 per cent of the list price.

- The distances are pro-rata, hence a car available for only one month but travelling 1,500 business miles in that time will attract a charge at the 18,000+ business miles rate.

- There is a reduction in the charge of 25 per cent where the car is four or more years old at the end of the tax year in question.

- If you are obliged to make a contribution to your employer towards the cost of your private motoring, this is deducted from the scale charge.

- The scale charge is reduced if the car is unavailable for private use for 30 consecutive days or more.

- The provision of a second car (e.g. for a spouse) is charged at 35 per cent of list price, unless more than 18,000 business miles are travelled, when this is reduced to 25 per cent.

A new regime will apply for 2002/03 onwards based on vehicle emissions. Environmentally friendly cars will be taxed at 15 per cent of list price rising to 35 per cent for the gas guzzlers. There will be no reductions for high business mileage.

What is the Fixed Profit Car Scheme?

Where an employee uses his own vehicle for company purposes, he will obviously look to his employer for reimbursement for his expenses. But how should he be claiming? There are two possible ways:

- either by the laborious process of allocating total vehicle expenses per year between business and private use, and then reclaiming the business proportion from the employer;

- or by the much easier method of using the Fixed Profit Car Scheme rates (FPCS), which show the maximum mileage rate that can be paid tax free;

The rates are shown in the table below and are fairly self-explanatory but the following illustration may help.

If an employee with his own 1,500cc car on which he personally pays all the expenses were to do a total of 5,000 miles in a year on company business, he could be paid 35p per mile for the first 4,000 miles (£1,400) and 20p per mile for the next 1,000 miles (£200). In total he could be paid £1,600 tax free.

The employer may register his scheme with his local Tax Inspector to avoid having to account for FPCS business mileage on an employee's form P11D. But in practice, most employers do not actually register but make the payments according to the scheme and show the full amount on the employee's P11Ds, with a note that the amount paid is at the

FPCS rates. The employee must remember to make a claim on his annual Tax Return stating that the full amount paid is 'wholly, exclusively and necessarily' for company business.

The employer should require the completion of an expense form to back up the claim that the mileage was for business purposes.

The Fixed Profit Car Scheme, provides these tax-free allowances per mile for business travel, i.e. one's own car used for employer's purposes:

| Business mileage for 2001/2 | Engine size | | | |
	Up to 1500cc	1501–2000cc	Over 2000cc	One rate
Up to 4,000 miles	40p	45p	63p	42.5p
Excess over 4,000 miles	25p	25p	36p	25p

There will be new rules for 2002/03.

If I am an employer and provide an employee with a car, what is the tax position?

To begin with, the employee will be taxed on the list price of the car according to the table in Appendix 1. Then there may be an additional tax charge on the fuel you, as an employer, pay for.

Remember that if you pay the taxable benefit charge on company fuel it is an 'all or nothing' charge. Either the employee pays for all his private petrol (including travel from home to work) and there is no tax liability on the fuel, or he or she pays tax on the full scale charge. Paying for part of private petrol will not reduce the tax payable on the scale charge one iota.

Can I get dispensation for travel and subsistence payments?

Most employers will have had the annual chore of having to complete the dreaded forms P11D dealing with employee benefits.

Although it is not possible to avoid making returns for genuine benefits (including company cars) it is possible to apply for dispensation from reporting travel and subsistence payments made to employees, so long as some fairly innocuous conditions can be met (receipts are requested, expenses are incurred in the course of business, mileage rates are within Inland Revenue guidelines and all claims are checked by a senior employee).

How do I provide a pension scheme for my employees?

Stakeholder Pensions are now the best bet. They have been on sale since 6 April 2001. Employers of five or more employees will have to offer access to a Stakeholder Pension, unless they already make adequate pension provision for them. There is now a clear distinction between schemes that offer benefits by reference to the amount of the contribution and those that depend upon measurement of final salary or length of service. It is the former that are represented by personal pension schemes and stakeholder schemes. The latter comprise the traditional form of occupational pension.

Stakeholder Pensions are supposed to be cheap and flexible – maximum annual charges of no more than 1 per cent of the annual value of the fund; minimum contributions of no more than £20 a time. Contributions are made net of basic rate Income Tax by the employee and gross where the employer decides to contribute.

What are the rules if I provide shares and share options for my employees?

Under the new Employee Share Ownership Scheme, employees may allocate part of their salary to shares in their employer company ('partnership shares') without paying tax or National Insurance contributions (NICs), nor are employers' NICs payable. Employers may also give free shares to employees, including extra free shares for employees who have partnership shares ('matching shares'), and the cost of the shares and of running the scheme are tax deductible. There are maximum limits of £1,500 salary per year for partnership shares and £3,000 worth of free shares per year, although employers may set lower limits.

If the employee takes shares out of the Scheme within five years, he is taxed under Schedule E. If the shares remain in the Scheme for five years or more, they are free of tax and National Insurance contributions when they are withdrawn.

There are two types of share option scheme: 'save as you earn' (SAYE)-linked share option schemes and company share option plans. Under an SAYE scheme, contributions of between £5 and £250 per month are paid under a SAYE contract with a building society or bank. The option will normally be able to be exercised after three, five or seven years when the contract ends. No charge to Income Tax arises on the difference between cost and market value when a share option is exercised, nor at the time it is granted.

The scheme enables an option to be granted now to acquire shares at today's price. The price at which the option may be exercised must not normally be less than 80 per cent of the market value of the shares at the time the option is granted.

Under approved non-savings-related share option schemes, the option must not be granted at a discount and the total market value of shares that may be acquired under the option must not exceed £30,000. If these conditions are complied with, there is no tax charge when options are granted. Nor is there a tax charge when the option is exercised, providing options under the scheme are exercised between three and ten years after they are granted, and not more frequently than once in three years.

What National Insurance is payable on employees' benefits?

If you are an employer and you complete form P11D for any of your employees, it is likely that there will be a Class 1A National Insurance liability arising on the benefits.

The amount of Class 1A NIC payable is calculated by reference to the value of the benefits provided and the application of the category A secondary Class 1 percentage rate in force. Calculation of the Class 1A NIC liability will be possible from the information contained in the new-style P11D form.

Payment of the Class 1A NIC will be due by 31 July following the end of the year in question, i.e. 31 July 2001 for 2000/2001.

Reading Inland Revenue booklet CWG5 is recommended and this also contains details of further sources of information.

What do employers and employees have to do at the year end?

Employer

The employer must complete forms P14/P60, form P35 and forms P11D/P9D. The employer must also ensure that all payments of PAYE tax and NIC have been paid over to the Collector of Taxes and any Class 1A NIC due for the year will subsequently be payable. The deadlines for these various items are as follows:

- Month 12 payment to the Collector of Taxes to avoid interest   19 April
- Providing the P60 to your employee   19 May
- Submitting the P14 and P35 to the Tax Office   19 May
- Making the Class 1A NIC payment to the Collector of Taxes   6 July
- Submitting forms P11D/P9D to the Tax Office   19 July

Employee

You should keep safely your P60, as it is not possible to replace it. You should keep evidence of any income that you have received during the year and any tax that you have paid. This is not limited to your employment and includes all of your tax affairs as a whole.

What are the rules for charitable giving through the PAYE system?

If an employer participates in the Payroll Giving scheme, an employee can authorise the deduction of whatever sum he chooses from his earnings before tax, for passing on to charities chosen by him, through a charity agency with which the employer has made an arrangement. The employee thus receives full tax relief for the contributions made.

What tax is payable on payments for compensation for loss of office?

Compensation for loss of office and wages in lieu of notice are both taxable when provided for in the terms and conditions of the employment. Also, if the payment is of deferred earnings, this too, is taxable under the normal PAYE rules.

Provided that the payment is not caught by the normal PAYE rules, the first £30,000 of the redundancy payment is exempt from tax. Any surplus received over and above this is treated as earnings and PAYE applied in the normal way.

Statutory redundancy payments, whilst not taxable in themselves, are included within the £30,000 exemption.

Payments for death or disability in service are not taxable. Lump sums received under approved pension schemes are also exempt from tax.

What are the tax rules if I am employed outside the UK?

If your employment abroad is full-time, spans a complete tax year and you actually carry out all your duties abroad, you are normally treated by concession as non-resident from the date of leaving and as a new resident when you return. If you do not attain non-resident status you will therefore be a UK resident throughout.

If you visit the UK, to retain non-resident status your visits must not add up to 183 days in any tax year, or average 91 days per tax year over a four-year period. Overstepping these limits will result in you being treated as resident and ordinarily resident in the UK.

The benefit of attaining non-resident status is that you escape UK tax on all of your earnings abroad.

What are 'fixed deductions'?

These are flat-rate expenses for employees, to cover the cost of tools, special clothing, etc. not provided by their employer. The amounts are mostly agreed with trade unions and do not preclude further claims, if justified.

Chapter 5

Pensioners and tax

What sort of state pension can you expect?

If you ring up the Contributions Agency giving them your National Insurance number, they should be able to send you a forecast of your anticipated state pension at retirement which they will work out based on your age and contributions to date.

What pension schemes are available for the employed?

Apart from the state pension scheme which one is forced to contribute to through being employed, you may either join your own company's pension scheme (if they run one) or you can contribute to your own pension plan, called a personal pension plan.

You should consider taking advice from an *independent* financial adviser on which pension scheme to contribute to. Salesmen of proprietary plans are very keen to promote their own brand for the simple reason that the more of their own products they sell, the greater their commission and the greater their take-home pay.

What pension schemes are available for the self-employed?

If you are self-employed, while you will be paying into your state pension by means of your National Insurance contributions (assuming you are paying them) you won't have any other pension scheme available unless you are paying into one. You are strongly advised therefore to consult an independent financial adviser to set you up with a scheme most suitable for yourself. The same comment that we make in the previous answer applies – watch out for commission-hungry salesmen.

What are free-standing additional voluntary contributions?

These are additional contributions made by an employee to his employer's approved pension scheme. They can be regular or they can be irregular.

How much can I pay into a pension scheme?

Your employer may operate an occupational pension scheme. If you contribute to such a scheme you should be receiving tax relief at source – i.e. no further action should be needed so far as your Tax Return is concerned (if you do not contribute to the scheme, then there is no annual relief due to you in any event).

If you make additional voluntary contributions you may do so up to 15 per cent of your salary, etc. each year. These are paid net of basic rate tax and if you are a higher rate tax-payer you will receive the extra relief by filling in the appropriate boxes on the Tax Return.

Personal pension scheme

To pay into a personal pension scheme you need to have relevant earnings – these could be from an employment where there is no pension scheme to which you belong, or from self-employment. See below for the contribution limits.

What are the new rules for carrying forward of pension contributions?

It is no longer possible to carry forward unused relief. Instead, there is a more generous scheme for working out the maximum relief for contributions in any year. Relief is now given up to a maximum of the greater of the 'earnings threshold' for the year and the 'maximum amount' for the year. The earnings threshold is £3,600 per annum. The maximum amount is calculated by reference to the 'basis year'. Net relevant earnings in the basis year may be used to 'frank' contributions for up to five years afterwards. The basis year is the year you choose from the five previous years. It can fall within the five years of the start of the stakeholder regime.

Retirement annuities

No fresh retirement annuity contracts have been written since 30 June 1988, but if you are still paying into one:

- the contributions are paid gross
- see the table below for contribution limits

Contribution limits

Age at start of year of assessment	% of net relevant earnings	
	Personal pensions	Retirement annuities
Under 36	17.5	17.5
36–45	20	17.5
46–50	25	17.5
51–55	30	20
56–60	35	22.5
61 and over	40	27.5

N.B. For personal pensions, there is a maximum sum you may contribute – see the Inland Revenue's own notes.

Is it worth paying into a pension scheme?

Now here is a very interesting question. Over the years of our being in practice, we have discovered that a number of our clients don't wish to pay into a pension scheme – they think they can do better investing on their own, either through clever investment or investing in property, etc. If you invest in a pension scheme, there is tax relief that goes with the payment of the contributions. However – and we are not the only people to say this – there is a case for funding your own pension in your own way and avoiding commission and all sorts of other complications that go with it such as keeping track of the tax position and possibly finding that the fund has been badly administered.

What are directors' pension schemes?

A limited company may well decide to run a pension scheme simply for the directors. There are generous contribution allowances, nearly all of which are deductible in the company's accounts and, on top of that, if there is a large fund in the directors' pension scheme, this money can be used to fund other business activities. In our view, directors' pension schemes are well worth looking into.

What are Stakeholder Pensions?

Stakeholder Pensions are new low-cost private pensions, available from 6 April 2001. They are meant for people who currently do not have a good range of pension options available, to save for their retirement.

If you earn more than £30,000 per year and are in a company pension scheme you cannot take out a Stakeholder Pension as well. Everyone else can have a Stakeholder Pension, even non-taxpayers, non-earners and children. Contribution limits are based on earnings but even if you have no earnings you can pay up to £2,808 into a Stakeholder Pension and this will be topped up to £3,600 by the Government.

Employers with more than five employees have to provide access to Stakeholder Pensions with effect from 6 October 2001.

Chapter 6

Self-employment and partnerships

Telling the taxman if you are going self-employed or starting a partnership

When you begin self-employment it is very important that somebody (you or your accountant) tells the Inland Revenue that you have begun in business, partly so that the correct tax can be paid on time and partly so that the appropriate National Insurance contributions are paid. Anyone beginning self-employment or a partnership must register with the Inland Revenue (which now incorporates the Contributions Agency) within three months from the end of the month in which the self-employment commenced. Failure to meet this deadline can result in a £100 penalty.

There are two forms which you should complete for the tax authorities, 'CWF1 Notification of Self Employment' and 'CA5601 Application to Pay Class 2 Contributions by Direct Debit', obtainable from any Inland Revenue office. However, please bear in mind that if your profits or share of profits for 2001/02 are below £3,955 then you will not have any Class 2 contributions to pay and you should inform the Inland Revenue accordingly.

Self-employment worries can be taken care of (and avoided) if you choose an accountant to handle your accounts and to advise you about the resulting tax liabilities.

What is trading?

It is sometimes difficult to know if an activity is taxable or not. Typical (in other words difficult) questions might be as follows:

- if I earn £300 a year from self-employed activities does the taxman want to know?

- my daughter, who is still at school, earns £50 a week from singing in local pubs; does the taxman want to know?

- I occasionally do small jobs for people, being paid in cash; will the taxman want to know?

It is always difficult to give the right answer because, while we know that under law if you are earning money the taxman will want to know, even if there is no tax to be paid, there is that famous maxim, which we cover elsewhere in this book 'de minimis non curat lex', which means the law is not concerned with trifles.

Trading is earning money from an activity. Trading involves not only the earning of the money but also the expenses in achieving that income. Our advice to clients is, and by using the template we show in Appendix 5, see if there is a taxable sum and if there is you should report it. Your conscience will tell you if you should be reporting it.

When an activity is in the grey area of being between non-reportable and reportable, each case has to be taken on its merits and decisions arrived at accordingly. However, in principle, once one is trading (earning money from an activity) proper records should be kept and the Inland Revenue told.

How do I calculate my taxable income from trading?

Basically, you have to take your income and deduct from it all your legitimate business related expenses. You will see the type of expenses that you can claim in Appendix 5 and you will see these listed in more detail below. However, do bear in mind that some expenses, for instance motoring, may well involve an element of private use. You should only claim that element that relates to the business activity against your trading receipts. It may be that you should only claim a third of your motoring costs against your business. Perhaps a quarter of your Council Tax and insurance costs. Whatever it is, if you have any difficulties in deciding, either go and see a local accountant or visit the Tax Office and discuss it with them.

A template to help you prepare your figures for the self-employed part of the Tax Return is provided at Appendix 5.

What expenses can you claim?

Basic costs and general running expenses

Normally allowed – Cost of goods bought for resale and raw materials used in business. Advertising, delivery charges, heating, lighting, cleaning, rates, telephone. Rent of business premises. Replacement of small tools and special clothing. Postage, stationery, relevant books and magazines. Accountants' fees. Bank charges on business accounts. Fees to professional bodies. Security expenditure.

Not allowed – Initial cost of machinery, vehicles, equipment, permanent advertising signs – but claim capital allowances. Cost of buildings. Providing for anticipated expenses in the future.

Use of home for work

Normally allowed – Proportion of telephone, lighting, heating, cleaning, insurance. Proportion of rent and Council Tax, if you use part of home exclusively for business – claiming ground rent and Council Tax, may mean some Capital Gains Tax to pay if you sell your home – but unlikely.

Wages and salaries

Normally allowed – Wages, salaries, redundancy and leaving payments paid to employees. Pensions for past employees and their dependants. Staff training.

Not allowed – Your own wages or salary or that of any business partner. Your own drawings.

Tax and National Insurance

Normally allowed – Employer's National Insurance contributions for employees. Reasonable pay for your spouse, provided he or she is actually employed.

Not allowed – Income Tax. Capital Gains Tax. Inheritance Tax. Your own National Insurance contributions.

Entertaining

Normally allowed – Entertainment of own staff – e.g. Christmas party.

Not allowed – Any other business entertaining.

Pre-trading

Normally allowed – Revenue business expenditure incurred within five years before starting to trade.

Gifts

Normally allowed – Gifts costing up to £50 a year to each person so long as the gift advertises your business (or things it sells). Gifts (whatever their value) to employees.

Not allowed – Food, drink, tobacco or vouchers for goods given to anyone other than employees.

Travelling

Normally allowed – Hotel and travelling expenses on business trips. Travel between different place of work. Running costs of own car. Whole of cost if used wholly for business, proportion if used privately too.

Not allowed – Travel between home and business. Cost of buying a car or van but claim capital allowances.

If a business leases a car costing more than £12,000, part of the leasing cost is disallowed for tax purposes. The rules are complicated but, in principle, the more expensive the car you lease, the smaller the sum that you will be allowed to claim as a tax deduction in your accounts.

Interest payments

Normally allowed – Interest on overdrafts and loans for business purposes.

Not allowed – Interest on capital paid or credited to partners.

Hire purchase

Normally allowed – Hire charge part of instalments (i.e. the amount you pay less the cash price).

Not allowed – Cash price of what you are buying on hire purchase (but you may get capital allowances).

Hiring

Normally allowed – Reasonable charge for hire of capital goods, including cars.

Insurance

Normally allowed – Business insurance – e.g. employer's liability, fire and theft, motor, insuring employees' lives.

Not allowed – Your own life insurance.

Trade marks

Normally allowed – Fees paid to register trade mark, design or patent.

Not allowed – Cost of buying patent from someone else but you may get capital allowances.

Legal costs

Normally allowed – Costs of recovering debts, defending business rights. Preparing service agreements. Appealing against rates, renewing a lease for a period not exceeding 50 years (but not if a premium is paid).

Not allowed – Expenses (including Stamp Duty) for acquiring land, buildings or leases. Fines and other penalties for breaking the law.

Repairs

Normally allowed – Normal repairs and maintenance to premises or equipment.

Not allowed – Cost of additions, alterations, improvements but you may get capital allowances.

Debts

Normally allowed – Specific provisions for debts and debts written off.

Not allowed – General reserve for bad or doubtful debts.

Subscriptions

Normally allowed – Payments which secure benefits for your business or staff. Payments to societies that have arrangements with the Inland Revenue (in some cases only a proportion). But watch for possible National Insurance contributions.

Not allowed – Payments to political parties, churches, charities contributions (but small gifts to local churches and charities may be allowable).

Travelling and subsistence expenses and tax

Expenses	Employer	Self-employed	Can VAT (input tax) be reclaimed?
	Where expenses are incurred by the employer	Where a self-employed trader incurs these expenses	
Entertaining own staff	Allowable	Allowable	Allowable**
Business travel between place of business and customers, etc. (but not home)	Allowable	Allowable	If charged, allowable
Hotel bills, etc.	Allowable	Allowable	Allowable, so long as it is billed to the VAT registered trader
Drinks and meals away from home:			
1. Working/selling	Allowable	Not allowable	Allowable**
2. On training course	Allowable	Allowable	Allowable**
3. Buying, etc. trips	Allowable	Allowable	Allowable**
*Entertaining business clients:**	Not allowable	Not allowable	Not allowable
Car parking	Allowable	Allowable	Allowable
Phone calls home	Allowable	Allowable	Allowable
Trade show expenses	Allowable	Allowable	Allowable
Petrol	Allowable	Allowable – business proportion only	Allowable***

*But a hotelier, restaurateur or someone who entertains in the normal course of his trade may claim these.

**But not if there is any measurable degree of Business Entertainment.

***But, if the input VAT is reclaimed, remember to include the scale charge in your OUTPUT TAX on the VAT Return.

Can I pay myself?

The answer to this is no. If you look at this logically you will see how the answer can only be no. If you were to pay yourself a salary out of your self-employment or partnership income you would have to include it as employment income elsewhere on your Tax Return and thereby you would achieve nothing.

Under this section you could also consider whether you could pay your spouse. If he or she plays a part in the business and has no other income, then there might well be tax to save by paying them for the work that they do.

What is the tax significance of holding trading stock?

If you are running a business that involves the buying and selling of items of stock, at the end of your trading year you have to add up the cost of any unsold stock and deduct it from the cost of your purchases acquired during the year. The reason for this is that those stocks are going to be sold in the following accounting period and therefore you only take advantage of the tax relief that goes with buying those stocks in the year or period in which they are sold. In other words any stocks that you deduct from your cost of sales at the end of your trading period should be added to the costs that you incur in the following year, so that you claim the deduction in the correct year.

What is the tax significance of work in progress?

If you are a builder and you have been working on a long contract, the duration of which straddles the end of your accounting period, you are likely to have incurred costs in terms of labour and materials at the end of your year which relate to that contract and which you have not been paid for. Accordingly you should value those materials, as well as those hours and, as with stocks, deduct them from the costs of that contract and carry the sum forward to the following year so as to take advantage of those costs in the year in which you receive the money for the work. This is a complicated area and we do recommend that you take advice from either the taxman or a local accountant.

Do remember that, in assessing the value of work in progress, if you are a partner or a sole proprietor in a business, you do not need to include your own time. But you do need to include materials.

What are debtors and what do I do about them?

Debtors are sums owed to you by your customers, but which have not been paid at the end of your accounting period. Even though you have not been paid you do have to include these as receipts due to you. If any of them have subsequently proved to be bad (i.e. you are not going to be paid), you can deduct from your debtors a figure relating specifically to the ones that are not going to be paid.

Come the next accounting period, and when that cash comes in, you don't pay tax on that money, because it has already been taxed in the previous year.

What are creditors and what do I do about them?

Creditors are like debtors but the other way round: they are the sums that you owe that you have not paid by the end of your financial year. You are allowed to include these sums in your accounts, and get the tax relief for them in the year to which they relate. However, when you come to pay them in the following year, you will not be entitled to tax relief in that year because you have already got the tax relief in the previous year.

What are capital allowances and agricultural and industrial buildings allowances?

You are unable to claim depreciation, at whatever rate you charge it, in your accounts as a tax deduction. Instead you have to claim, and in a prescribed way, the Inland Revenue's own version of depreciation. You will almost certainly need professional help to do this properly. These allowances are specifically allowed as a deduction against your taxable profits. You claim them as follows:

Plant	Capital Allowances
Machinery	Capital Allowances
Motor Cars	Capital Allowances
Fire Safety Equipment	Capital Allowances
Agricultural Buildings	Agricultural Buildings Allowances
Industrial Buildings	Industrial Buildings Allowances

Is there any special tax treatment for farmers?

Apart from the fact that farmers will be able to claim agricultural buildings allowances in addition to normal capital allowances, there are two specific ways in which farmers get special tax treatment:

1. **The herd basis.** In recent years, this has been less of an attraction as a means of saving tax because the value of farm animals has fallen during this period. However, the principle of herd basis is that, because a herd, or a flock for that matter, consists of breeding animals (cows, bulls, rams, ewes) instead of treating these as animals that you will ultimately sell as meat, you treat them as capital assets and not as a revenue item. This book on tax is not the place to describe this particular feature but the effect of claiming herd basis at a time of rising animal values is that, when you come to sell those animals (perhaps retire), a substantial part of the sale proceeds will not be subject to tax.

2.   **Averaging.** Because farm results can fluctuate, farmers are able to claim the averaging of profits of any pair of consecutive years of assessment provided they do so within broadly 22 months of the end of the second year. As with herd relief, the rules can be quite complicated but the effect of claiming for averaging is that you can collectively pay less tax than you would if you had a very high profit attracting higher rates of tax in one year and a loss or lower profits in the adjacent year.

Is there any special tax treatment for visiting sports stars and entertainers?

The bad news is that UK appearances by non-resident sportsmen and entertainers are taxed at once. Payments of £1,000 or more are subject to basic rate Income Tax at source. The good news is that it is possible to agree a lower or nil rate with the Inland Revenue authorities where it can be established that the eventual United Kingdom tax liability will be less than basic rate.

Is there any special tax treatment for Lloyd's insurance underwriters?

Yes, there is special treatment for Lloyd's underwriters. It is such a complicated set of rules, allowances and revisions that our advice is to say, as succinctly as possible, go to a specialist adviser who deals with Lloyd's underwriters.

Is there any special tax treatment for subcontractors?

Construction Industry Scheme – the new rules

Anyone affected by this should know the following basic new rules:

1.   This only applies to those who work in the construction industry.

2.   If you work in the construction industry you will need either a registration card CIS4 (for you to be paid net of tax) or a certificate CIS6 (if you want to be paid gross).

3.   You will need to get your registration card or certificate in place as soon as possible.

4.   Since 1 August 1999, forms 714, 715 and SC60 have not been valid.

5.   The easiest document to obtain will be the registration card – i.e. payment to you will be net of tax. To get a registration card you simply have to work in the construction industry, be able to prove your identity and fill in the form to get the card from the Tax Office.

You will continue to prepare accounts for your business and, all things being equal, if you have received a tax refund in the past you should continue to receive a tax refund in the future.

6. If you want a subcontractor's tax certificate (if you want to be paid gross) you have to pass each of three tests:

    (a) Turnover test – you must have a net turnover – i.e. sales less cost of materials of at least £30,000 – in three of the last four years. For partnerships the net turnover figure of £30,000 is multiplied by the number of partners. For a new business, you must have a total turnover of £21,000 in any six consecutive months leading up to the date of application.

    (b) Compliance test – you must have kept your tax affairs up-to-date for the last three years, including paying your tax and National Insurance on time and always operating the construction industry scheme correctly. If you have incurred any tax penalties you are likely to fail this test.

    (c) Business test – you must own your own stocks. You must own your own equipment. You must keep proper books of account and you must operate from proper business premises.

7. While this may sound frightening, in our opinion it is fair, reasonable and straightforward. Particularly because taxpayers always like receiving refunds of tax, most people who are affected by this, so long as they obtain the registration card CIS4, should not encounter too many problems.

Is there any special tax treatment for owners of mineral rights and royalties?

If you receive income from mineral rights or you are an author or composer by profession, then your receipts will be taxed as part of your professional earnings and you will be able to deduct more expenses than otherwise would be the case. In principle, you pay tax in the year in which the mineral rights or royalties are received, but there are rules for spreading royalty receipts over a number of years and, should you fall within this case, we strongly advise you to seek professional advice. We emphasise this particularly after the Budget statement on 7 March 2001, when the Chancellor announced significant changes in the area.

How do I get tax relief for losses in my business?

Trading losses may be:

- relieved against income or gains of the same year;
- relieved against income or gains of the previous year (however, you must claim the full loss, up to the total income for that year);
- carried forward against future profits of the same trade

Are there any special rules about claiming farm losses?

Because a number of wealthy people used to claim the substantial losses they made through their farming activities against their other substantial income, the Inland Revenue said that they would limit the number of years for which someone in this category could go on claiming farming losses.

How many years of farm losses can one utilise before having to carry forward those losses?

Five. A loss in the sixth tax year of a consecutive run of farming losses can only be relieved against later profits of the same trade. In recognition of the current dire state of many farmers' finances, this rule has recently been relaxed for 2000/01 and 2001/02 by concession in certain cases. Once you have made a farming profit then the five-year sequence starts again.

The figure of loss or profit is arrived at before claiming capital allowances.

What is Class 4 National Insurance?

If you are trading, and your profits exceed £4,535 you have to pay 7 per cent Class 4 National Insurance contributions on the figure of your profits above £4,535 with an annual upper earnings limit of £29,990. The maximum Class 4 National Insurance contribution payable by a self-employed person in 2001/02 is £1,775.55.

What is a partnership?

A partnership is a formal business arrangement entered into by two or more people whereby the profits and losses of a business are shared in agreed proportions.

In order for the Inland Revenue to be happy that a partnership exists, they will want to see a number of the following items before they will agree to tax the business as a partnership:

- a partnership deed;
- the names of both partners on bank statements;
- the names of both partners on business letterheadings and other printed stationery;
- some sort of evidence that both parties agreed that there should be a formal partnership between them.

Do you need to have a partnership deed?

Our advice to any partners is that there should be a partnership deed so that, if anything should happen to one of the partners, or they should fall out, there is a legal agreement entered into at the start which establishes how the partnership should be dissolved and how the assets and liabilities allocated.

Perhaps, where there is a partnership between husband and wife (and this is often not a good idea for a great number of reasons) it is not that essential to have a partnership deed, but in every other case that we have come across we have always recommended that the parties go to a solicitor and draw up a proper partnership deed. Alternatively, Law Pack publishes a Partnership Agreement F211.

What are limited liability partnerships?

An Act creating a new corporate business vehicle, the limited liability partnership (LLP) has recently made its way through Parliament. This will allow organisations the flexibility to enjoy limited liability while organising themselves (sharing profits, etc.) as partnerships. The LLP will be a separate legal entity. It will be governed by agreement between the members (an incorporation document). Nevertheless, it will be required to disclose, to Companies House, similar information to that required of companies. It will, however, be taxed as a partnership.

We look on this development with some interest because we now regard the limitation of liability as being more theoretical than real. When companies fail, in our experience, the directors often have to pay up on previously given guarantees and if the company has failed through maladministration, then directors and quasi-directors can be sued as private individuals.

In principle, we think LLPs are a good thing, but in practice we don't think it is going to make much difference to anybody.

What happens if partners change?

If partners change, when the partnership Tax Return is completed and the ratio of agreed profits or losses for the year in question is allocated to the varying partners (whether static, incoming or outgoing), that share is shown clearly on the partnership deed and the individual partners themselves pay the tax that their share attracts.

How are partnerships taxed?

Partnerships have their own Tax Return. The accounts are entered into the relevant boxes on the partnership Tax Return and, on the back pages, the profits are allocated between the partners in the agreed proportions.

In addition the partnership must prepare individual sheets called either Partnership (Short) or Partnership (Long) depending on the nature of the income that the partnership earns, and these individual sheets are handed to the partners themselves for attaching to their own individual personal Tax Returns.

In other words, partnerships don't pay tax. It is the partners who pay tax on their share of the profits.

What happens about partnership capital gains?

If a partnership makes a capital gain it is included on the partnership Tax Return and the share of the capital gains must be added to the individual partner's personal Tax Returns so that they themselves pay tax on their share of the gain.

How long do I have to keep my accounting records?

There is a legal requirement to keep accounting records for six years.

How might the Inland Revenue inquire into my tax affairs?

Under the new regime, the Inland Revenue are entitled to investigate for one of three reasons; either –

1. they think a minor point is wrong and needs to be corrected; or
2. they don't like the look of the accounts and suspect that there may be something fundamentally wrong; or
3. the nasty bit, a Tax Return may be selected at random.

When a letter arrives from the Inspector of Taxes, you can't tell which of the three has triggered the process. So, just because your accounts may be investigated, don't get worried. Sooner or later everyone will have an investigation.

Chapter 7

Income from
land and
property

What is the wear-and-tear allowance?

This applies to furnished lettings only. It is normal for taxpayers in receipt of income from land and property to claim all their allowable expenses (see Appendix 8 for a template for identifying those expenses) against income. However, instead of claiming for the cost of renewing furniture, furnishings and fixtures such as cookers, dishwashers or washing machines, taxpayers are entitled to charge a 10 per cent wear-and-tear allowance instead. This 10 per cent allowance is calculated as being 10 per cent of rent received, less Council Tax and water rates paid (see below).

In our experience it is usually better to claim actual repairs – they usually amount to more than the deduction that the wear-and-tear allowance will give you – and so we do urge taxpayers to keep proper records of all expenditure incurred in connection with their land and property income.

How do I claim losses from land and property?

There is a difference between the tax treatment of a land and property loss and a trading loss. Losses from land and property income can only be carried forward and set against profits in subsequent years from land and property.

The only exception to this is if you have any losses on furnished holiday lettings; as that is treated as a trade, you may offset such losses against your other income or capital gains in the same year or the previous one.

Furnished lettings and furnished holiday lettings

Furnished lettings

If you receive income from furnished lettings it is taxed under Schedule A – i.e. income from UK land and property.

Instead of keeping a record of all your repairs you may, if you wish, claim a wear-and-tear allowance which is worked out as being 10 per cent of your rent less 10 per cent of your Council Tax.

i.e.	Rent	£1,000
	Council Tax	£200
	Rent less Council Tax	£800
	Wear-and-Tear Allowance @ 10% = £80	

However it is usually more tax-effective to claim actual repairs.

If you provide: laundry, meals, domestic help, etc. for your tenants, then you may be able to claim that are running a self-employed business – such as you usually can if you are providing holiday lettings (see below). The advantage of running your property enterprise as a business means that there are usually more expenses you can claim against tax, and you may be able to use part of any annual surplus to provide you with a pension.

Holiday lettings

If you let out holiday accommodation, the definition of furnished holiday lettings is:

- The accommodation must be available for holiday lets for at least 140 days.

- The accommodation must be let for 70 days.

- No let to exceed 31 days.

The income is treated as earned income (a trade) attracting Capital Gains Tax, rollover relief, retirement relief and taper relief.

Tax saving ideas worth thinking about...

- Rollover of capital gains on the sale of trading assets into the purchase of holiday accommodation.

- Any gain on the sale of the holiday accommodation may eventually attract CGT at only 10 per cent.

- You can claim capital allowances on furniture and equipment.

- If you make a trading loss from your holiday lets you may offset it against your other income or capital gains in the same year or the previous one.

However...

- Don't buy the accommodation with a substantial mortgage because the Revenue may regard your motives as not being commercial.

- Don't forget about the VAT consequences, if you are VAT registered.

Rent-a-room – income from lodgers/B & B

If you let a room in your house and you are an owner occupier, or a tenant who is sub-letting, the first £4,250 of any income is tax free – i.e. a rent of £81.73 per week is tax free.

If the rent is higher than £4,250 you either elect to pay tax on the surplus above £4,250 (without relief for expenses) or you can treat the arrangement as being furnished lettings and prepare accounts.

Woodlands – what are the rules about selling timber?

There is no Income Tax charge on woodlands; neither woodland rents nor timber is taxed. There is no charge to Capital Gains Tax on trees that are standing or felled. In other words, proceeds of sale of timber are not taxed at all.

Dealing in property

You may find, perhaps because you are a developer, that you carry out a number of purchases and sales of land and buildings and that, instead of these transactions being treated as falling within the Capital Gains Tax regime, the profits and losses you make are caught under the Income Tax regime. There are some taxpayers who have been badly caught by this and in principle it is quite difficult to give a hard-and-fast rule as to when somebody moves from the Capital Gains Tax regime to the Income Tax regime. However, all may not be lost, because when a capital asset falls within the Income Tax regime, not only are the losses more favourably treated but also there are usually more expenses that can be claimed as well.

In our opinion you should seek professional advice if this eventuality comes to pass in your case.

How are lease premiums taxed?

Lease premiums are now becoming 'more a thing of the past' but if you do grant a lease of not more than 50 years duration, for which you receive a premium, then you will be assessed to Income Tax on the premium. The taxable amount is quite complicated to calculate but (putting a block of ice on your head we will try to explain it): you take the premium and reduce it by 1/50th of its amount for each complete period of 12 months, other than the first, and that is subject to Income Tax. The balance of the premium is normally subject to Capital Gains Tax.

Chapter 8

Income from dividends and interest

How are dividends taxed and can I claim the tax back?

The means of taxing dividends from shares has changed since 6 April 1999. Before that date it was possible, under the right circumstances, to claim a refund of the tax deducted on the dividend. Now that is no longer possible.

The new rules are somewhat complex: the old rate of tax on dividends of 20 per cent has now become 10 per cent and, again unlike the old system, the company does not have to pay the 10 per cent over to the Inland Revenue and it is for this reason that the tax, not having been paid, is not refundable to the shareholder under any circumstances by the company paying the dividend.

In our view the new system is more complicated than the old. The old system did need revising but we firmly believe that the Chancellor of the Exchequer got it wrong when he introduced this new system.

The effect of this is that the number and size of tax refunds taxpayers can claim each year has dropped dramatically.

How do I pay the tax on interest I receive that is not taxed at source?

Most interest is taxed at source and if at the end of the tax year too much tax has been deducted from a taxpayer's income, the tax suffered on interest payments can be refunded.

However, in some cases interest is paid gross and under those circumstances the gross interest has to be reported on the tax return and any under- (or over-) payment of tax worked out on the tax calculation sheets.

What is the tax position on bank interest?

Most bank interest is now paid net of tax. Taxpayers in receipt of interest from a bank should ask that bank to send them a certificate at the end of the tax year showing the gross interest, the tax deducted from it and the net figure. Those three figures will be entered on the Tax Return, either on their own or when added to other net bank interest figures.

What is the tax position on building society interest?

Building society interest is very much like tax on bank interest (see above). Some building society interest is paid gross, in which case no tax repayment is possible; but if you have a building society account and have received net interest, at the end of the tax year you should ask them to send you a certificate of interest paid.

Please note that building societies often send statements of interest paid. The statement does not constitute a certificate and so if you wish to have tax repaid to you, you will need to ask your building society to issue you with a certificate of interest paid.

What is the tax position on annuities?

Annuities are sources of income usually enjoyed by the elderly. The taxpayer makes an investment in the annuity and over the remaining period of his or her life receives payments in connection with this annuity, some of which is capital and some of which is taxable. When the annuity is paid it will be clearly shown how much is capital (and this is not taxable) and how much is income and how much tax has been deducted.

You should total the interest elements of each payment (gross, tax and net) and enter them on your Tax Return.

What are Personal Equity Plans?

Personal Equity Plans (PEPs) were no longer issued after 6 April 1999. They provided an attractive way to invest in equities and unit trusts, etc., and they also carried Capital Gains Tax exemption.

They were replaced by ISAs (Individual Savings Accounts) on 6 April 1999.

What are TESSAs?

TESSAs stood for Tax Exempt Special Savings Accounts and were introduced in January 1991. They were free from Income Tax and were very competitive. However, with effect from 6 April 1999, as with PEPs, they were replaced by ISAs and therefore no longer available.

What are ISAs?

ISA stands for Individual Savings Accounts. They are not as attractive as PEPs and, like the proverbial camel, were obviously dreamt up by a committee. There is an annual contribution limit of £5,000 but they are Income Tax- and Capital Gains Tax-free. The subscription limit is £7,000 for the year 2001/02.

Why are ISAs not as attractive as PEPs and how do they differ?

Like PEPs, ISAs are free of Income Tax and Capital Gains Tax. Where ISA investments are in shares, dividend tax credits will be paid into the account for the five years to 5 April 2004. But these tax credits are only one-ninth of the net dividend compared with one-quarter under PEPs. Under PEPs, you could invest £9,000 per annum in shares but, under ISAs, the figure is only £7,000.

All UK residents over the age of 18 can open such an account. The Government will provide a 10 per cent tax credit each year for the first five years on dividends from UK equities that are invested in an ISA.

As we have said, the maximum investment in the first and second years will be £7,000 of which not more than £3,000 may be in cash (e.g. National Savings, bank deposits, etc.) and not more than £1,000 in life insurance. However, in both instances you can invest up to the annual maximum fully in stocks and shares, now £7,000 in 2001/02.

Husband and wife both have their own limits. There will be no penalty for withdrawals at any time. Although if you subscribe the maximum amount in a year and then withdraw sums you will not be allowed to replenish the account until the next tax year has started.

There are two types of ISA – Maxi ISAs and Mini ISAs. A Maxi ISA enables savers to spread their money between cash deposits, shares and insurance in a single plan run by just one finance company. In the case of Mini ISAs, you may use one financial service provider for shares, another for cash and a third for insurance, etc. but you cannot have a mix of Mini and Maxi ISAs being started in the same tax year. As we said before, it is unnecessarily complicated but if you want to make the maximum investment in stocks and shares you will need to have a Maxi ISA.

What are Venture Capital Trusts?

Venture Capital Trusts were introduced to encourage individuals to invest indirectly in unquoted trading companies. If you do this you will be exempt from tax on dividends and capital gains arising from shares acquired of up to £100,000 a year. In addition, income tax relief of 20 per cent applies on up to £100,000 in any tax year, if you subscribe for new shares which you then hold for at least three years.

What are Enterprise Zone Investments?

Enterprise Zone Investments should not be confused with the Enterprise Investment Scheme. There may be an element of overlap, but the point of Enterprise Zones is that they tend to be areas of high unemployment that are given special tax breaks.

Enterprise Zones are of more interest to those who wish to set up businesses in them and professional advice should be sought. The Enterprise Investment Scheme is a scheme giving tax breaks to investors in unquoted trading companies.

Chapter 9

Life assurance policies

What do I need to know about the taxation of life assurance?

The answer to this is probably 'not very much'. Life assurance used to enjoy a highly favoured tax status, but since 1984 this has been reduced. Some benefits remain and the overall concept is dealt with below.

There are three main types of life assurance. Firstly there is **term assurance**, the sum of which is only paid if you die during the term of the policy; there is no savings element in this policy, but they tend to be cheap. Secondly there is **whole of life assurance**, whereby the sum is payable on your death at any time and the third policy is an **endowment policy** where the amount assured is payable on your death within the term of the policy or at the policy's end.

If you invest now in a life assurance policy (normally called 'single premium bonds') you will pay no basic rate Income Tax when you draw the money out from it. However, you may be liable to the balance between higher rate tax 40 per cent and the basic rate tax 22 per cent if certain circumstances apply.

If what follows sounds complicated, don't worry, because the life assurance company is bound to send not only you but also the Inland Revenue a certificate detailing the information about your policy and the gain that you have made.

In principle, if you withdraw no more than 5 per cent of your investment each year, there will be no further tax implications on this sort of policy. If you withdraw more than 5 per cent there may be tax to pay, but we do suggest that rather than going into the complicated calculations in this book, you should take advice from either the Inland Revenue or a qualified accountant.

What are chargeable events?

A chargeable event is when you withdraw money from a life assurance policy or bond. As you will see from the previous question, unless you withdraw more than 5 per cent of your investment in any Tax Year, there will be no tax implications.

What are bonds?

There are all sorts of bonds, including Euro Bonds, Guaranteed Income Bonds and Single Premium Bonds. The subject of Euro Bonds does not really fall in the scope of this book, but in the case of Guaranteed Income Bonds these resemble annuities and only the income element is subject to Income Tax.

In the case of chargeable income bonds, we refer you to the question above relating to the taxation of life assurance where we hope you will find the answer.

What is 'top slicing relief'?

Top slicing relief is complicated and we do suggest that, if you want a full answer which you will properly understand, you either attend the local Tax Office or refer to a professional adviser. Basically, it is a relief available to individuals (but not to companies) against what otherwise would be a higher rate of tax on any investment gain you might make on surrender or sale of a life assurance policy.

What are 'partial surrenders'?

If you make a partial surrender of a life assurance policy, and this is usually the case when you receive annual payments from a single premium bond, it may give rise to tax but only if you withdraw more than 5 per cent of your original investment.

As with areas of this chapter on life assurance policies, we recommend you to take professional advice, because the explanation of this complicated area of the tax law is beyond the ambit of this book.

Can I claim tax relief on my permanent health insurance payments?

Permanent health insurance policies are intended to provide you with an income, should illness prevent you from working. If your employers pay the premium on your policy, they will obtain a tax allowance on the payment they make and you will have to pay tax on any benefit that you receive.

If you make the payments, whether as an employee or as a self-employed person, you will not obtain any tax relief, but any benefits paid to you under these circumstances would be tax free.

What are 'purchased life annuities'?

Purchased life annuities are investments normally taken out by the elderly which receive favourable tax treatment, but do contain substantial risk.

The basic principle is that you invest a lump sum with an insurance company; then each year, up until the day of your death, they will repay part of the capital together with interest. The interest is taxed but the capital is not. This is one way of increasing the spendable income of elderly people. However, the danger is that if an annuity is taken out on day one and the annuitant dies on day two, all the money is lost.

Chapter 10

Capital Gains Tax

What is Capital Gains Tax (CGT)?

If you make a gain on the sale of any investments, land and buildings, jewellery, antiques, or any form of other property, you may be liable to Capital Gains Tax.

What does CGT catch and what does it not catch?

The main activities that we, as accountants, see our clients paying Capital Gains Tax on are as follows:

- Sale of investments
- Sale of antiques over £6,000
- Sale of property
- Gifts

Here is a list of some of the assets that are exempted from the Capital Gains Tax net:

- Private motor vehicles
- Your own home (but not including a second home)
- National Savings Certificates
- Foreign currency
- Decorations for gallantry (unless purchased)
- Betting winnings (including pools, lotteries and Premium Bonds)
- Compensation or damages for any wrong or injury suffered
- British Government Securities
- Life assurance policies and deferred annuities
- Chattels (i.e. movable possessions) sold for £6,000 or less
- Assets given to a charity or the nation
- Business Expansion Scheme shares
- Timber and uncut trees
- PEPs
- Venture Capital Trust shares held for five years
- Enterprise Investment Scheme shares held for at least five years

A rough guide to Capital Gains Tax is provided at Appendix 8.

What are the new rules since 6 April 1998?

The Chancellor, Gordon Brown, introduced some complex changes to the Capital Gains Tax (CGT) legislation in the 1998 Budget. The rules were already overcomplicated for such a low yielding tax but Mr Brown appears to have made things worse. Please note these rules apply only to individuals, partnerships and trusts. Companies soldier on under the old rules, claiming indexation allowance after 5 April 1998. Here are the main changes:

- Indexation relief is frozen at April 1998; for assets held since 1982 this means an uplift of approximately 104 per cent on 1982 values, but with no further indexation post April 1998.

- From April 1998 taper relief has been available to reduce gains on all assets, giving more relief for business than non-business assets. The taper operates on a time basis by identifying complete years of ownership post April 1998 (with a bonus year for post 5.4.98 disposals of non-business assets where owned before 17.3.98). Ten years achieves a maximum relief of 40 per cent for non-business assets (four years and 75 per cent for business assets) giving eventual maximum tax rates of 24 per cent and 10 per cent respectively on chargeable gains. Taper relief is complicated, especially where the gain attracts both indexation and taper relief; professional advice should be sought.

- Losses will be deducted from gains before taper relief and losses can be offset against gains with the lowest taper in preference to other (higher taper) gains. 'Bed and breakfasting' has been effectively abolished (although there are variations which can still apply) by bringing in a 30-day matching rule.

- Capital Gains Tax re-investment relief has been restricted and rationalised.

- Retirement relief is being phased out – this will severely damage the less well off person who is retiring in favour of the significantly better off (a curious example of New Labour favouring the rich!).

Who pays Capital Gains Tax?

The quick answer is: the person making the gain; but where an asset is given away and the taxpayer may think that he has made no gain (because no money has been received) and therefore has no tax to pay, he may easily be mistaken. Because a gift constitutes a disposal, if there is a gain on that disposal, even the giver, who is in receipt of no income, pays Capital Gains Tax on the gain that they are deemed to have made on the disposal.

To pay Capital Gains Tax one has to be a UK resident taxpayer, which includes a company, trust or partnership.

However, if you are not domiciled in this country, you are only charged Capital Gains Tax on your overseas realisations of assets when you bring the money here.

Is there an annual exemption from Capital Gains Tax?

Every year there is an annual exemption from Capital Gains Tax and in the year 2001/02 your first £7,500 of gains is exempt. In the case of trusts, it is £3,750. As we have said, if you sell a chattel, the maximum sale proceeds of which is £6,000, you don't pay any Capital Gains Tax.

The rate of Capital Gains Tax is, for individuals, either 20 or 40 per cent and for trustees and personal representatives it is 34 per cent.

What can I set against my Capital Gains Tax liability?

Apart from the annual exemption, you are entitled to set the costs of both acquisition of the property, including purchase price, and the sale or disposal, against the gain.

In addition, if you bought an asset on which you have incurred enhancement or improvement expenditure, then that too will be allowed as a cost. Certain costs such as accountant's fees are not allowed but, if you are looking for allowable costs, and because this subject can be so wide ranging, we suggest you talk to either a professional accountant or to the Inland Revenue.

What is 'indexation'?

Up until 5 April 1998, you were allowed to set against any capital gain the element of that gain which was caused by inflation. In other words, you didn't pay tax on inflationary gains. The amount that you could set against your gains, called indexation, was the amount by which the retail price index had increased between date of acquisition and date of disposal. One needed to look at tables to work out the indexation, but in principle, in respect of an asset that was sold in 1988 or afterwards, indexation had the effect of increasing the allowable costs.

Since 6 April 1998, indexation has no longer been an allowable deduction, although it is still available for companies. Note this doesn't mean you can't claim indexation; it is just that the gain that has arisen since 5 April 1998 cannot be indexed.

What is 'taper relief'?

Taper relief is the new relief that was introduced by the Government with effect from 5 April 1998 which applies to gains realised after that date, subject to the rules. According to the number of completed years that the asset has been owned after that date, only a percentage of the gain will be chargeable and is shown in Table 2. Please note that any non-business assets you acquired before 17 March 1998 and disposed of after 5 April 1998 attract an extra year for taper relief purposes.

Our view is that the new system is very complicated. In the past, as practising accountants, we could work out very quickly in our heads roughly the Capital Gains Tax bill should a client telephone wondering what the tax would be if they were to sell their mother's house, or this or that investment. Now the rules are so complicated (because one has to use both indexation and taper relief) that only mathematical geniuses can work out the tax quickly. We strongly advise you to take professional advice or see if the Inland Revenue can process your query quickly.

Table 2. Capital Gains Tax taper relief

Gains on disposal of business assets		Gains on disposals of non-business assets	
No. of whole years in qualifying holding period	Percentage of gain chargeable	No. of whole years in qualifying holding period	Percentage of gain chargeable
0	100	0	100
1	87.5	1	100
2	75	2	100
3	50	3	95
4	25	4	90
5	25	5	85
6	25	6	80
7	25	7	75
8	25	8	70
9	25	9	65
10 or more	25	10 or more	60

Can I get any relief for capital losses?

If you sell or give away a capital asset at a loss, it is normally deductible from any capital gains that you have made during the same year and any remaining unrelieved losses are available to carry forward against future capital gains.

However, there is some relief available from a different quarter. If you make a loss in your trade or profession and do not have enough income to cover it, you can elect for the unused losses from that trading period to be set against your Capital Gains Tax for that same tax year. In other words, Capital Gains Tax can be reduced by trading losses. Again, we would suggest that you seek professional advice or help from the taxman on this.

How and when is CGT paid?

Capital Gains Tax is payable on 31 January following the end of the tax year in which the gain was made. The tax payable is included with your Income Tax calculation working sheets after you have worked out your Income Tax payment.

What are the rules for part-disposals?

Where part of an asset is disposed of, you have to work out the cost applicable to the part sold.

The rules are complicated. A special rule applies to small part-disposals of land and provided that the sale proceeds do not exceed one fifth of the total market value of the land you may deduct the sale proceeds from your base cost rather than pay any tax now.

What are the rules for private residences and CGT relief?

Normally, the house or flat in which you live is exempt from Capital Gains Tax when you sell it. The property must have been your only or main residence during the period of ownership. The last 36 months of ownership is ignored for this purpose. You can also be absent for periods totalling three years and for any period throughout which you worked abroad. In addition, if you had any work which required you to live in job-related accommodation, that also does not stand against you for Capital Gains Tax purposes. Any periods of absence in excess of the periods allowed result in the relevant proportion of your sale profit being charged to Capital Gains Tax.

If a specific part of your house is set aside for business purposes then that proportion of your profits on sale of the house will be taxable. However, if you do not have any rooms used exclusively for business purposes you will not normally be liable to any Capital Gains Tax if you sell your house.

Special consideration needs to be given to houses with a lot of land alongside them. If land is sold in excess of what the Revenue regard to be a normal area of garden in character for the house that is being sold, then part of any gain on the sale of such extra land will be subject to Capital Gains Tax.

If you owned two properties, within two years of buying the second one you should have sent in a letter (called an 'election') in which you disclosed to the taxman which you were treating as your private residence for Capital Gains Tax purposes. Otherwise, the taxman will decide for you.

What are the rules for chattels sold for less than £6,000?

A chattel is an asset which is 'tangible movable property', such as a work of art or a set of chairs. Provided that the asset fetches no more than £6,000, the Inland Revenue do not require you to pay Capital Gains Tax on it. However, if you have a set of dining room chairs and while each one is not worth £6,000 but in total the set is worth say £30,000, the set will attract Capital Gains Tax on it, because a set is treated as a chattel.

What CGT relief is there for disposal of business assets?

In principle, you are liable to Capital Gains Tax in respect of any assets used in your business. But if further business assets are purchased within one year before or three years after the sale, you can claim 'rollover relief' as a result of which the gain on the disposal is deducted from the cost of the new business assets acquired. So no tax is paid until the new business assets are sold, unless they too are replaced. For these assets to qualify they must either be land and buildings, fixed plant and machinery, milk and potato quota or other agricultural quotas. Please note that motor vehicles or any vehicle on wheels do not qualify.

What CGT relief is there for gifts?

In principle, gifts of assets do not escape Capital Gains Tax, but business gifts relief enables the following to attract a special relief called 'holdover relief':

- Business assets
- Agricultural property
- Shares and securities in a family trading company
- A gift which gives rise to an immediate charge to Inheritance Tax

Such gifts which attract IHT are rare, but one such example is when you transfer assets into a discretionary trust. Gifts to individuals and to accumulation and maintenance settlements, or to trusts for disabled people, are classed as potentially exempt transfers (PETs) and IHT will not be payable, unless you die within seven years of making the gift. However, tapering relief may reduce the IHT payable after three years.

How do I claim retirement relief?

The rules for retirement relief have changed and the very generous reliefs are now being restricted in accordance with Table 3. In principle if you sold a business, you could claim up to £250,000 retirement relief for Capital Gains Tax purposes and between £250,000 and £1 million you could claim 50 per cent relief on the gain that fell in that band. But, as the Table shows, the relief will no longer be available at all from the year 2003–2004.

Table 3. Withdrawal of retirement relief

Year	100% relief on gains up to (£):	50% relief on gains between (£):
1998–99	250,000	250,001–1,000,000
1999–00	200,000	200,001–800,000
2000–01	150,000	150,001–600,000
2001–02	100,000	100,001–400,000
2002–03	50,000	50,001–200,000

What are the aspects of CGT if I live abroad?

If you are resident and ordinary resident in this country, you are liable to tax on any capital gains realised anywhere in the world. But if you have realised a gain in a country which will not allow the proceeds to be sent to the UK you can claim for the gain to be deferred until the year in which you receive the money in this country.

If you are non-resident in this country but are carrying on a trade in the UK, you are liable to Capital Gains Tax on the assets used in the business. If you are UK domiciled, the Inland Revenue do have new powers to apportion certain capital gains of overseas trusts of which you are a beneficiary and this has caught out a number of wealthy people who transferred their assets abroad.

If you leave the UK for tax residence abroad you must be absent for at least five years if you wish your capital gains in the UK or abroad to be UK tax free. This is a complicated matter and professional advice should be sought. The table in Appendix 9 may help.

Chapter 11

Trusts, etc.

What is a trust?

A trust is brought into existence when a person (called the 'settlor') transfers some of his or her assets to trustees (who become the legal owners) for the benefit of third parties, called beneficiaries; a trust is a legal entity in itself. Another word for a trust is a settlement. Sometimes trusts are created under a Will and sometimes they are created during the lifetime of the settlor. Sometimes trusts are created to save tax, sometimes to protect assets; there are many and various reasons for setting up a trust.

Does a trust have to complete a Tax Return and what tax does a trust pay?

Trusts, or rather trustees, do have to complete a Tax Return reporting their income and capital gains on an annual basis, although this is often prepared by a solicitor or accountant. In cases where trusts are formed on the death of the settlor (in this case called testator) the appropriate lower rate of tax is paid by the trustees and the beneficiaries are treated as having paid the tax that has been deducted by the trustees.

In the case of discretionary trusts (and again we are verging into the area where professional advice should be sought) sufficient extra tax must be paid to bring the total tax up to 34 per cent, which is the basic rate for discretionary trusts.

The tax the trusts pay is paid on 31 January and 31 July each year.

How are trusts in Wills affected by tax?

The main tax that affects Wills, triggered by the death of the person, is Inheritance Tax and there is a separate section in this book dealing with this very aspect. However, when someone dies their personal representative or executor will make sure that a personal Tax Return is completed from the start of the tax year to the date of the deceased's death. From the date of their death to the end of the tax year the personal representative (PR) will have to account for tax and report to the beneficiaries on the tax that they have deducted. Each year the PR will have to submit an Income Tax Return to the Inland Revenue. However, in the year in which the estate is wound up and all the assets have been distributed, the PR will only have to account for the tax on the income up to the date of distribution.

What are accumulation and maintenance settlements?

An accumulation and maintenance settlement is a settlement normally created for the benefit of a minor where the income from a trust is accumulated and not distributed until the beneficiaries reach the age of at least 18. The income from such trusts attracts tax at 34 per cent.

What are discretionary trusts?

A discretionary trust is one in which the settlor gives discretion to the trustees as to how they treat the income and capital and to whom they distribute it. These trusts also pay Income and Capital Gains Tax at the rate of 34 per cent.

How do discretionary trusts pay Inheritance Tax?

A discretionary trust does not pay IHT on a death, but it does pay IHT on every tenth anniversary of the date of settlement if this was after 31 March 1983. The charge, called the periodic charge, is at 30 per cent of the lifetime rate, which is itself half of the rate on death. In principle, the rate of tax is therefore 6 per cent (i.e. 30 per cent × 20 per cent) of the assets in the trust, but the calculation is not an easy one and you should seek professional advice.

How do trusts pay Capital Gains Tax?

Most trusts attract half the annual exemption that is available for individuals. This is currently half of £7,500 i.e. £3,750 (for 2001/02). The capital gains are worked out in accordance with the usual Capital Gains Tax rules (see Chapter 10) and the tax on any capital gain is paid over at the same time as the balancing payment for the Income Tax, in other words 31 January following the end of the tax year.

Chapter 12

Corporation Tax

What is Corporation Tax?

Corporation Tax is the tax that limited companies and unincorporated associations (such as clubs) pay on their profits. It is a tax on the profits of the company; profits include interest and capital gains.

How is Corporation Tax assessed and paid?

Corporation Tax is accounted for in 12-month periods, unless the accounting period from its commencement to the first accounting date, or the last period of operation, is less than 12 months. (You may already be thinking that it is time to consult a professional accountant and, in our view, if you have a limited company and you are dealing with Corporation Tax you should certainly seek professional advice.) Every company has to fill in an annual Corporation Tax Return (form CT600) and this Return has to be submitted by the company secretary or the directors within 12 months of the end of the accounting period. However, tax has to be paid, assuming we are dealing with a small company, nine months after the end of the accounting period. Big companies have to pay Corporation Tax at more frequent intervals.

How are company profits calculated?

In principle, company profits are calculated in the same way as profits for non-incorporated businesses. However, this book does not pretend to be the only tool you need to calculate your company's profits properly.

What do I have to do about the Corporation Tax Return?

When the Corporation Tax Return arrives, we strongly suggest you send it to your accountant and get them to complete it for you. This will normally be done once the accounts have been prepared.

Do companies pay more or less tax than the self-employed?

This is one of those 'It all depends...' answers. If you don't want or need to withdraw the profits your company makes, then the top rate of tax companies pay is less than the top rate of tax paid by an individual. However, if you withdraw the profits, in the form of a dividend then you are effectively switching the company profits into your own hands. There is no extra tax to pay if you are a basic rate taxpayer, but there will be an extra

22.5 per cent if you are a higher rate taxpayer. If you withdraw the profits as salary then the tax rate increases further due to the National Insurance charge that will have to be paid. In our office we have a general rule that, for a husband and wife partnership, it is probably not worth incorporating their business until the profits reach £100,000.

What is the rate of Corporation Tax and how does the small company rate of tax work?

There are three rates of Corporation Tax but the way they work is complicated and the rates and limits are by no means fixed. The rates are as follows:

- Starting rate of 10 per cent – for profits up to £10,000. Where profits exceed £10,000, the rate of tax increases dramatically by a process called 'marginal relief'. If your company's profits are above £50,000, you will not benefit from this lower rate.

- Small companies rate 20 per cent for profits up to £300,000. Where profits exceed £300,000, again the rate of tax increases dramatically by marginal relief. If your company's profits are above £1,500,000 you will not benefit from this lower rate either.

- Full rate 30 per cent.

When is a company trading and how does this affect its tax position?

A company is trading once it has sold something. It is also trading if it has been incorporated and has begun to develop and manufacture goods or services. Any loss that it makes will be carried forward until it makes its first profit. The loss can then be used to reduce the first profits.

Do dormant companies have to pay Corporation Tax?

Dormant companies are, by definition, those that are doing nothing and although a Corporation Tax Return has to be submitted, there would be no tax to pay.

Under recent legislation it is possible for a dormant company to do certain minor things (such as issue shares and pay the annual return fee), but this does not constitute the earning of taxable profits.

What are 'associated' and 'subsidiary' companies?

Associated companies are those that are under common control or where one controls the other.

A subsidiary company is one that is either wholly or substantially owned by another company.

What is the significance of a 'close company'?

A close company is, broadly speaking, a company that is under the control of five or fewer 'participators'. A participator is a person having a share or interest in the capital or income of the company. It is defined broadly to include, for example, any loan creditor of the company and any person who possesses a right to receive or participate in distributions of the company. A quoted company is not a close company if more than 35 per cent of its voting shares are owned by the general public.

Close companies used to be subject to special provisions, but the only provision that applies now is where they make loans or distributions to their directors. When this happens tax has to be charged on the loan or distribution, unless the loan is repaid before the tax is due.

What is the difference between a public and a private company?

A public company is a company limited by shares or guarantee, having a share capital and:

- the Memorandum of Association of which states it to be a public company;
- that has been registered as such;
- whose name ends 'public limited company' or plc;
- which has an allotted share capital of not less than £50,000 of which at least 25 per cent has been paid on issue.

All other companies are private companies. A private company that incorporates some but not all of these features remains a private company.

Note: Although private companies have advantages over public companies, trading under any sort of incorporated structure attracts serious administrative and some tax disadvantages. Professional advice must be sought.

What do UK companies with overseas income have to do about it?

A company that has overseas income has to pay Corporation Tax on the gross amount of such income, but double tax relief is usually available. If a UK company receives a dividend from an overseas company from which tax has been deducted, as we have said, the gross dividend is included in the taxable profits. However, there are other rules and we do suggest that you refer to specialist advice for help.

What are the tax rules about companies buying their own shares?

In the case of a small company, it is frequently difficult for a buyer to be found for the shares of a shareholder who wishes to retire or sell up. There are now rules which enable companies to buy their own shares but, once again, we suggest that professional advice is sought on this. Briefly, the rules are:

- that the company must not be quoted and should be trading or be the holding company of a trading company;

- the purchase of the shares by the company must be mainly to benefit the trade of the company;

- the shareholder must be UK resident and must have owned the shares for at least five years. In addition, his shareholding must be substantially reduced and this usually means by at least 25 per cent;

- if the payment is used to pay Inheritance Tax, within two years after death the above provisions do not apply.

How do I pay myself from my company?

In principle, you can either pay yourself a salary (which could be in the form of a bonus or other remuneration) or, so long as you hold shares in the company, you could be paid a dividend.

If you are paid a salary, normal PAYE rules apply. If you are paid a dividend, the company does not have to pay any tax over at the time of making the distribution. This is because dividends can only be paid out of profits which have already been taxed. In principle, dividends are now a more tax-efficient way of withdrawing profits from a company than salary. But don't forget that, if you have lent money to your company and that company wishes you to be able to withdraw some of that loan (to have it paid back) there would obviously be no tax involved with any such repayment.

What are the tax rules about a company paying dividends?

If a company pays a dividend, since 6 April 1999 it no longer has to pay any tax (called Advance Corporation Tax) over to the Inland Revenue. In the old days, this tax used to be used to reduce the eventual Corporation Tax due. Under the new rules, with no Advance Corporation Tax being paid the full sum of Corporation Tax has to be paid nine months after the end of the accounting year.

In the hands of the shareholder, the tax credit which is included on the dividend voucher is not available for a refund, but it does count for all the tax that has to be paid by basic rate taxpayers.

How does a company get relief for its losses?

This is a large subject but we will try to give the basic rules as simply as we can.

A loss made in an accounting period can usually be carried back against the profits for the preceding year or, if the loss occurs in the year before a business ceases trading, the loss can be carried back for three years. Otherwise the loss is carried forward and set off against the profits of future years.

Where a company has subsidiaries, it is possible for the losses of one company to be set off against the profits of another company in the group (see below) (again professional advice should be sought).

How does group relief for losses work?

As we have seen in the previous question, the trading losses of members of a group of companies can be used to reduce the trading profits of other members of the group, provided that:

- a claim is made within two years of the end of the accounting period;
- the parent and subsidiary companies are all based in the UK and that the parent has at least 75 per cent interest in each of the subsidiaries.

Please note that even though the parent may only own 75 per cent of the shares, it is entitled to 100 per cent of the relief. Also note that capital losses cannot be group relieved.

There are complicated rules where a company joins or leaves a group during an accounting period – another reason for seeking professional advice.

How does a company pay Capital Gains Tax?

Companies pay Corporation Tax on their capital gains. Companies can still claim indexation relief but they do not enjoy the new tapering-relief.

Trading losses in accounting periods may be set off against not only gains, but also trading profits of the same period or indeed the previous period. Capital losses incurred by a company can only be offset against capital gains of the company in the same period or future accounting periods.

While capital losses cannot be group relieved if one company in a group has a gain, another company in the group may be able by prudent investment to offset the gain in the other company by claiming rollover relief. This is complicated and professional advice should be sought.

Can a director borrow money from his company?

In principle, a director cannot borrow money from his own company unless tax is accounted for on it. Small expense sums are allowed to be borrowed in advance, but if a substantial sum is borrowed not only does tax have to be paid on the sum borrowed (this sum is repaid by the Inland Revenue when the loan is repaid), but in addition, interest has to be paid on the beneficial effect of enjoying what is normally an interest-free loan. The short answer to this question is 'no'.

Do companies claim capital allowances, agricultural and industrial buildings allowances in the same way as sole traders and partnerships?

The normal capital allowances rules for businesses apply to companies, but there are special rules and we suggest that professional advice is sought.

Chapter 13

Non-residence, working overseas, etc.

What is the significance of my tax domicile?

Your domicile is the country which you regard as your natural home and the place where you intend to return in the event of going abroad. For most people it is the country of their birth and, unlike tax residence, it is not possible to have two domiciles under English law.

The point about domicile is that if you are tax resident in this country but domiciled abroad, you don't have to pay Capital Gains Tax on your overseas gains until that money is remitted to the UK.

What is the significance of my tax residence?

Your tax residence is fixed by your circumstances of where you live and, when the figures and dates are worked out, how the Inland Revenue interpret your residence.

If you have always lived in this country you are treated as being ordinarily resident here.

If you have come to this country but intend to return to another, while the Inland Revenue will regard you as tax 'resident' they will not regard you as 'ordinarily resident' for tax purposes. Nowadays your residence position is not affected by your having a place of abode here. In other words, you may go abroad for a number of years to work and the fact that you still own a house in the UK does not mean that you are automatically considered to be a UK tax resident. If you wish to be considered as non-resident for tax purposes, you should spend a full tax year outside the country although short periods in the UK may be disregarded by the Revenue.

What income is taxable and where?

If you are resident in this country all normal taxable income, whether arising here or overseas, is taxable. However, if you are non-resident and you receive income from self-employment, partnerships or employment, all of which are carried out abroad, it will be tax free. If you are non-UK domiciled, on your death Inheritance Tax will not have to be paid on any of the assets that you own abroad.

The rules are complicated so any aspect that needs further consideration should be referred for professional advice.

What is 'double taxation relief'?

The UK Government has entered into agreements with certain overseas countries (about 100 in all), the purpose of which is to prevent income being taxed in both countries. So, where income has already been taxed in another country, in principle that counts towards your UK tax bill. However, such overseas tax is not refundable.

How do I change my tax residence?

In order to change your tax residence you could:

- Simply establish a permanent residence abroad and remain out of the country for a complete tax year (although in certain circumstances short visits are allowed).

- After that you must avoid returning to the country for as much as six months in any one tax year and this must average less than three months here in every year.

When does someone who goes abroad become non-UK tax resident?

In principle somebody going abroad does not become non-UK tax resident until the start of the tax year following his or her departure. In order to remain non-UK tax resident for that year, they have to stay outside the country for a full tax year.

What tax do I pay on foreign income?

If you are a UK resident you pay normal tax on income from abroad, but if any of that foreign income has already suffered Income Tax in the country of origin, then it is more than likely that double taxation relief will result in that tax going towards paying your UK tax bill. However the foreign tax cannot be refunded.

What tax do I pay on foreign pensions?

For people who are resident, ordinarily resident and domiciled in the UK, there is a 10 per cent deduction permitted from their foreign pension before calculating the tax liability which arises from it.

If the foreign pension is paid as a result of Nazi persecution, then no liability to UK tax arises.

What is the tax position on professions conducted partly abroad?

If you work in any profession that is conducted partly within this country and partly overseas, you will normally be assessed to UK tax on your entire profits and it is only if you conduct a separate profession entirely abroad that special rules will apply.

What tax do I pay on earnings from overseas employment?

Again this is a tricky area but, broadly, if you go to work abroad, so long as your absence lasts a whole tax year and your visits to the UK total less than 183 days in any tax year and on average are less than 91 days per year, you will not pay UK tax on your overseas earnings, and that includes your overseas earnings in the part of the tax year in which you leave the UK.

What allowances can non-UK tax residents claim?

You may be able to claim UK tax allowances if you are not resident here. If you are eligible to claim you will generally be given the same allowances (i.e. personal allowance) as an individual resident here. The following can claim:

- a resident of the Isle of Man or the Channel Isles
- a citizen of the Commonwealth
- a citizen of a state within the European Economic Area
- a present or former employee of the British Crown

and certain others.

If I go abroad, do I have to pay tax on the rent I receive from letting out my home while I am away?

Unless you apply to the Inland Revenue for a certificate authorising your agent to make payments to you without deducting tax, a letting agent must deduct tax at the basic rate from all remittances sent to you.

You will still be entitled to your personal allowance and it may be that some of the tax that is deducted can be refunded to you. We strongly suggest you employ the services of an accountant to look after this for you.

If you employ no agent you will have to pay UK tax on an annual Tax Return.

Can I go abroad to avoid Capital Gains Tax?

This is a complicated matter and professional advice should be sought, but if you leave the UK for tax residence abroad, you should complete five tax years before you can be pretty confident that any capital gains, whether arising in the UK or abroad, will not be subject to Capital Gains Tax.

What should I do if I have just arrived in the UK to take up work here and will the rest of my overseas income be taxed?

In principle, you should contact the authorities, or your employer will do this for you and from that day, even if it is the last day of the tax year, you will be entitled to the normal personal allowances. Equally from that day you will be subject to Income Tax and National Insurance rates because you will be treated as a UK tax resident.

If you are self-employed or have income arising from a partnership or self-employment abroad or indeed interest arising abroad, it is not normally taxed.

If I have just arrived in the UK, will the rest of my overseas income be taxed?

In principle, you will only pay UK tax on your overseas income that is remitted to the UK.

Should I put my money in an offshore trust?

The short answer is, 'No'. In 1998, new provisions were introduced whereby the UK tax payable by beneficiaries of trusts who are not UK-resident increased dramatically.

Foreign income and residence issues are summed up in table form at Appendix 9.

Chapter 14

Inheritance Tax

What is Inheritance Tax?

Inheritance Tax (IHT) is basically the old 'death duties'. At one stage some years ago it was also called Capital Transfer Tax. However, Inheritance Tax was introduced in the 1986 Finance Act and, although it is a highly complicated tax, certain basic information should be included in this book.

IHT covers transfers not only on death, but certain lifetime transfers as well, particularly to discretionary settlements. However, lifetime transfers are only normally taxed if the death of the transferor occurs within seven years of making the transfer.

It is well worth bearing in mind that, starting at 40 per cent, Inheritance Tax is reaping far more for the Treasury than it used to and so this is a tax which should be attended to and where possible planning to minimise it should be put in place.

How and when is Inheritance Tax paid?

Inheritance Tax is due at the date of someone's death. However, if a transfer is made which attracts inheritance tax during life, and that transfer is made between 6 April and 30 September, the due date for payment is 30 April in the following year. If the chargeable transfer is made between 1 October and 5 April, the due date is six months after the end of the month in which the transfer is made.

How should I approach the subject of Inheritance Tax?

As practising accountants we hardly ever deal with Inheritance Tax matters ourselves, but we have been able to observe the way in which it is dealt with by other professional advisers and we have some fairly strong views on the subject. Our view is that if you are worried about Inheritance Tax, on the whole, you should not go to a solicitor for advice but rather to a specialist Inheritance Tax adviser. While we don't like commenting on other professionals, we think that the following analysis is fair and appropriate. On the whole, chartered accountants are extremely competent at Income Tax, Capital Gains Tax, Value Added Tax as well as other accounting functions, but on the whole we should not advise our clients on matters of law. So that when it comes to solicitors, while they are very competent at matters of law, in our opinion only those who have the appropriate training and experience should advise their clients on matters of tax and particularly Inheritance Tax, where we have seen a number of bad mistakes made by people who have not been properly trained, who 'didn't know what they were doing'. So our advice is that Inheritance Tax planning should be dealt with by a specialist in Inheritance Tax matters. This is how we run our practice and how we advise our clients whenever they need Inheritance Tax advice.

Should I make a Will?

We always ask our clients if they have made a Will and try to make sure that, if they have not, they do so quickly. If you haven't made a Will the chances are that, when you die, your assets will not go to the people you would like them to go to. It is not expensive drawing up a Will and we would strongly suggest you go to a solicitor to do so. However, in view of our comments about Inheritance Tax planning, we think it would be a good idea for you to ensure, before you visit the solicitor, that you have listed your assets, applied a rough valuation to them and seen if the Inheritance Tax bill is one you are prepared to pay. If you are frightened by the size of the Inheritance Tax bill then we suggest that you go to an Inheritance Tax specialist and then, when you go to your solicitor, you can be armed with not only what you want to happen but how you want the Inheritance Tax matters to be dealt with. If you don't do it this way round you may find that you have a solicitor who thinks he knows about Inheritance Tax making all the plans for you and, as I say, in our experience this can often end in problems, and major problems. But you do need to make a Will.

A template to help you work out your IHT bill and plan to make a will is provided at Appendix 10.

How do I choose my executors?

In our view it is extremely important to appoint executors whom your survivors like. We have seen cases where the executors who have been appointed were not liked by the surviving spouse and the misery caused by the death of the testator was exacerbated by the insensitivity of the executors. So don't choose your own friends just because you like them. Make sure your spouse likes them too and is happy for them to be appointed.

How can I reduce Inheritance Tax?

This is such a big subject and the sums involved are so potentially enormous, that we would not presume to give anything more than general advice in a book of this nature. However, there are certain general rules which we believe to be sound:

1. Don't give everything away before you die; if you do and you keep on living what will you live on?

2. Try to make your Will match and mirror the Will of your spouse.

3. Money distributed to surviving spouses upon death is free of IHT. So try to give away the tax-free band (this varies each year) to people other than your spouse (assuming your spouse will have enough to live on if you do); anyway

it is as well to take advantage of the second available tax-free element on the first death.

4.   Consider leaving your estate to a discretionary trust. While Inheritance Tax will be payable on the setting up of the discretionary trust, on your death, your survivors will not pay tax again on those assets when they die.

5.   Consider taking advice from an Inheritance Tax specialist (as we keep on saying).

6.   Keep your Will up to date.

7.   Let your survivors know in advance if their lives are likely to be radically affected by your death. For instance, if you are a wealthy person and you wish to leave your money to somebody you don't see very often, it is not a bad idea to let that person know so that, in return for the anticipated inheritance, they look after you in your old age and are nice to you, etc. It is equally important to let those people know if you change your mind! There is this problem that Wills generate great anticipation and anxiety and it is as well not to be too secretive about what you are proposing to do, so as to reduce extra stress and burdens on your survivors after you have died.

What are periodic charges?

A discretionary trust is subject to a charge to inheritance tax every 10 years at 15 per cent of the scale rate of 40 per cent. Thus a 6 per cent charge is made every ten years on the assets in the Trust.

What is 'quick succession relief'?

If, after someone dies and Inheritance Tax is paid on their estate, a beneficiary dies within five years, quick succession relief applies and the tax payable on the second death is at a reduced rate.

How will assets be valued?

In principle, on death your assets are valued for Inheritance Tax purposes at what they might reasonably be expected to fetch on the open market.

Chapter 15

VAT

What is VAT?

Value Added Tax is a tax imposed when goods or services are sold. Any business which has a turnover in excess of £54,000 should, in principle, register for VAT and add VAT to its VAT-able supplies. VAT is collected by HM Customs & Excise rather than the Inland Revenue.

This is a complicated subject and anyone running a business with a turnover approaching £54,000 should seriously consider approaching an accountant and consider whether they should register for Value Added Tax with Customs & Excise.

In the case of businesses with a turnover in excess of £54,000, they certainly should take professional advice because they may be starting to get into deep trouble.

What records do I need to keep if my business is VAT-registered?

We strongly suggest that you keep records, either on a computer or in a cash analysis book; all your VAT records should be kept for six years.

In addition to this you do need to keep your invoices on which you have claimed back VAT input tax. You also need to keep copies of your sales invoices on which you have recorded your output tax.

You have to remember that it is likely that you will be investigated by both the Inland Revenue and the VAT officials more than once during the average life of a business. When they come to see you, they will be wanting to check that your accounts are in order and that your VAT Returns have been properly prepared. You should arrange your affairs in such a way that anyone can find their way from your original transactions through to the submissions to the Inland Revenue and Customs & Excise without too much difficulty. The technical term for this is an audit trail and we would strongly suggest that you ask a professional accountant for help in making sure that your records are complete and well-filed.

How do I complete my VAT Return?

For most VAT-registered traders, Customs & Excise need just four figures for the VAT Return:

1. Output VAT (box 1). This is the total of the VAT you have charged on your sales invoices during the period. If you complete the VAT return under the cash accounting rules (if your turnover is less than £600,000), then your output tax

is calculated on the cash received during the period and not on the invoices issued. The figure must include any VAT scale charge for private motoring.

2. Input VAT (box 4). This is the VAT that you yourself have paid during the period. If you are registered for VAT, then nearly all the VAT you have paid can be included in this box. However, you may not reclaim VAT on the purchase of motor cars and, if you reclaim VAT on fuel, then you must add the scale charge for your car in box 1.

3. Total ouputs (box 6). This is the sum of the invoices you have issued to your customers (the sales of standard and zero-rated goods and services) during the period. This sum should exclude the VAT element. However, if you are cash accounting, you total the sum received from your customers during the period but exclude the VAT element.

4. Total inputs (box 7). This is the total of the payments you have made for standard and zero-related purchases during the period, less the VAT element. You should not include any exempt purchases, nor any drawings.

You will notice that there are five other boxes on the VAT return:

- Boxes 2, 8 and 9 affect few small traders; if they affect you, you should seek professional advice.
- The only other boxes that affect everyone are boxes 3 (the total of boxes 1 and 2), and 5 (the sum of box 3 less box 4).

Lastly, remember that you must send back the completed Return, together with a cheque for any payment of VAT, before the end of the following month.

Chapter 16

Stamp Duty

What is Stamp Duty?

The most obvious area in which Stamp Duty bites is on the purchase of properties. Stamp Duty is also payable on transfers of shares and certain other documents and it is quite complicated trying to work out whether something attracts Stamp Duty or not.

We will begin with purchase of freehold property. The Stamp Duty payable by the purchaser is as follows (for transactions after 28 March 2000):

up to £60,000	–	Nil
over £60,000 and up to £250,000	–	1 per cent
over £250,000 and up to £500,000	–	3 per cent
over £500,000	–	4 per cent

When it comes to share transfers the amount of stamp duty payable is 50p for every £100 or part thereof. Stamp Duty is not payable on the issue of shares.

While on this subject it might be worth mentioning the subject of Capital Duty. This was abolished on 16 March 1988 and so need not concern the reader.

It might be helpful to include a list of the instruments which require stamping:

- Stock and share transfers
- Declarations of trust
- Certain proxy forms
- Tenancy agreements where the gross rent is more than £5,000 per annum and is for a six- or twelve-month term

Certain Stock Transfer Forms only attract a fixed duty of 50p, no matter what the transaction and these are listed on the Stock Transfer Form.

However, in spite of all the foregoing, transfers to, from or between trustees, transfers in connection with divorce, and transfers which are gifts do not attract Stamp Duty.

When and how is Stamp Duty paid?

Stamp Duty is assessed and paid by the person who is responsible for ensuring that it is paid. He or she sends the document to be stamped off to the Stamp Duty Office (your local Tax Office will tell you where this is) and the document will be returned to you stamped with the amount that you have paid.

If you happen to be in London it is well worth a visit to Bush House in The Strand to see the Stamp Duty Office, because in there you will see stamping machines which were made 70 years ago, still going strong. Maybe one day stamping will become electronic in one form or another, but at the moment it is performed by what can only be described as 'Green Goddesses'.

Chapter 17

Other tax issues

Tax planning 'do's'

- Buy your own house as soon as you can. Historically, houses have been a good investment. Any capital gain will be tax free. However, by the same token there are no tax allowances for any losses on sale.

- Make sure you have got good pension and life assurance cover and keep the situation constantly under review.

- Make use (if you can afford to) of the £3,000 tax free annual capital transfer (i.e. give this sum away Inheritance Tax-free each year) and, if you did not use up last year's allowance, you can give away an additional £3,000.

- Always claim your personal and other tax allowances. This should normally be dealt with for you by the Inland Revenue but you should keep the matter under annual review (i.e. have you passed retirement age?).

- Claim all business expenses you are entitled to against any business profits – always keep a chit for petty cash expenses. If you do not, how will your accountant know you have incurred that particular expense?

- Pay your spouse properly for any work he or she does in your business. In the 2001/02 tax year, remember, he or she can earn £4,535 tax free, although payments over £4,524 will involve him or her paying National Insurance contributions.

- Consult with your stockbroker in order to make sure you take advantage of the annual £7,500 Capital Gains Tax relief, i.e. if you can make a gain of this size it will be tax free.

- Make a Will. Consult Law Pack's *Last Will & Testament Guide* or take legal advice.

- Think carefully about providing funds to pay any Inheritance Tax on death (term assurance is not very expensive).

- Plan ahead and wherever possible let your accountant know of your plans/ wishes so that you can be advised on any tax implications.

- Divide your assets and income with your spouse so that the best use is made of the independent taxation rules.

- Let an independent financial adviser give you the equivalent of a financial 'medical examination'.

- Ask your accountant to give a rough idea of your tax liability in January and July each year. Then divide the sum by 12 and start saving up for it by transferring the monthly figure to a deposit account. This way paying tax is much less painful.

Tax planning 'don'ts'

There is a lot of what one might call pub chat about tax – particularly on the subject of avoiding tax – and quite often the apparent expert is not giving the full picture. This is our attempt to give the tax novice some basic tax information so that he or she can tell whether the information coming across the crowded smoke filled room (or wherever) is accurate.

1. Don't avoid receiving income because it will have to have tax paid on it. If you earn £1 and pay the taxman 22p you are still left with 78p and that is 78p more than you started out with. Whether you are prepared to do the work or whatever for a net benefit of 78p is another matter. The main argument, often put forward, that you will not be able to afford to pay the tax on any extra income is a false one. If you receive income and pay tax on it you are left with something. If you do not receive the income in the first place you will be left with nothing.

2. Don't put tax saving first. Always put sound commercial or family considerations first and then fit the tax implications into what you want to do. If you own a business which is making money and paying tax, the key fact is that your business is making money. If your business is losing money and paying no tax then, the thing to concentrate on is not how marvellous it is that you are paying no tax but how vital it is to turn the business around and start making money. In the same way, but on a personal level, do not emigrate to a tax haven in order to save tax. Emigrate to a tax haven if you wish but your reason for doing so must not be to save tax but instead because you would rather live there than in the UK. If you do not like the place why go to live there? Thus plan to do what you want to do first and then fit the tax implications into the picture.

3. Don't enter into tax saving schemes, whether on the advice of an accountant or anyone else, that run a long time. The law can change, your circumstances can change and either could make a nonsense of a long-term plan.

4. Don't automatically trust Trusts. Be very careful with putting your money into trusts – do not set them up unless they will do for you exactly what you want. Trusts set up to protect assets from the ravages of tax can result not only in tax having to be paid but also assets having to be sold to pay the tax. Net result being ghastly. Some trusts are very useful but tread very carefully. Take professional advice.

5. Don't give all your money away – in order to save Inheritance Tax. If you do what will you live on?

6. Don't make your affairs too complicated. Keep your affairs simple and flexible – so that you can (a) understand what is going on and (b) make any changes as and when you want.

7. Don't try to cheat the taxman. Be honest in all your dealings. Keep proper records of all your transactions, especially cash receipts, and declare everything properly. If you don't, you will be found out.

Tax-saving tips

For employers, employees and company directors

- Shares: companies can offer shares to staff through a share option or share incentive scheme. The rules are complicated but the chances of acquiring wealth in a tax efficient way are very real. Talk to an accountant first.

- Company car: this is still the most popular fringe benefit.

- Cheap loans to employees: in many case no taxable benefit arises in the case of a loan of up to £5,000.

- In general all benefits are taxable but meals provided free of charge (or at low cost) in a canteen on the firm's premises are not taxable if they are available to staff generally.

- The Inland Revenue's practice is not to tax expenditure of up to £75 per head on the annual Christmas party or similar function.

- Accommodation: a company may purchase a house for an employee to live in rent free. There may be a small amount of tax due on the value of the accommodation, etc., but the charge will be small in proportion to the benefits provided.

- Payments to private health care schemes, such as BUPA and PPP, are not taxable for lower-paid employees (defined as those receiving under £8,500 per annum, including the payments).

- Tax is not payable on financial rewards to staff for suggestions they may make on the running of a business. However, such 'suggestions schemes' must meet certain fairly minimal requirements.

- Incentive awards: employees can be given non-cash awards for meeting certain targets and, in addition, any tax that these might attract can be paid by the employer on the employees' behalf.

- Occupational pension schemes: while these speak for themselves and their benefits are well understood it is sometimes overlooked that employees may increase their pension entitlements by making additional voluntary contributions (AVCs) to the scheme. AVCs attract tax relief at the highest rate of tax. Employers could also consider making pension schemes non-contributory. This way they could reduce payments they make to staff by the amount of the pension contributions the staff members have been making (in other words the member of staff would be no worse off as a result of this) but the company would have less National Insurance contributions to pay on the lower salary figure.

- Company directors will be able to save themselves a little tax in the form of National Insurance contributions for themselves, if instead of receiving their pay in the form of salary they were to receive the equivalent sum in the form of rent for the company's use of property owned by the director, dividends on shares or interest from the loan made by the director to the company. However, you should seek professional advice.

- Loans to directors: it is illegal under company law for a company to lend any director money and, even if it is done, there are heavy tax penalties attached to this. Do consider the following points:

  (a) Immediately before incorporation the business could take out a bank loan enabling you to withdraw a substantial sum in advance.

  (b) You could arrange the capital structure of the company so that at least part of your investment is by way of a loan account against which you may be free to draw.

  (c) It may be possible to keep certain assets (e.g. property used by the business), outside the company.

- Other benefits: provide tax free benefits to your employees such as childcare, sports or recreation facilities.

For those moving house while changing jobs

If you move home in order to take up new employment, or even a new post within your existing organisation, the following costs can be re-imbursed by your employer without any income tax charge arising, up to an overall maximum of £8,000:

1. Bridging finance

2. Legal and professional fees, stamp duty, removal costs and insurance

3. Travel and hotel costs

4.   A reasonable subsistence allowance

5.   A disturbance allowance

For those about to retire or who are retired

Golden Handshakes – advance tax planning

- You might ask your employer to pay part of any payment over £30,000 into your pension rights (within the limits of the scheme). The Revenue accept that no tax charge arises on such payments and this could enhance the tax free lump sum you receive from the scheme.

- If you are retiring and your total income will be significantly lower after retirement it may be better to retire shortly after 5 April so that the taxable part of your Golden Handshake may be charged at a lower tax rate.

For the over 65s

- Do remember that age allowance (a higher personal allowance) is available for those aged 65, and for those over 75 there is a higher age allowance available.

For the self-employed

The self-employed have considerably more flexibility in their tax saving arrangements than employers and employees and those who are self-employed are probably well aware of the sort of advantages they may legitimately take – however, here are a few that should not be overlooked:

- Particularly for those starting in business and needing all the profits to live off, if possible, do not use a limited company. For the self-employed, the National Insurance rates are less, the flexibility is far greater and the administrative costs are considerably less.

- A personal pension scheme is a most efficient way of diverting surplus profits into a tax free lump sum and pension for the future.

A list of the types of expenses generally allowed is on pages 49 to 52.

For personal taxpayers – particularly higher rate taxpayers

For those with high income (i.e. into 40 per cent tax band), and particularly if it is surplus to requirements, funds can be diverted to the following havens for tax advantages either on initial payment or at a later date:

- Life Assurance – investing in a 'with profits' endowment policy that will run for at least ten years does produce a good tax-free return.

- National Savings Certificates – these still produce a good tax free income. It is always a good idea to keep aware of what National Savings schemes have on offer.

- Perks in quoted shares – many quoted shares now offer perks to their shareholders and these are entirely tax free.

- National Insurance – there is a maximum total of National Insurance contributions you need pay. If you have more than one source of employment earnings and you are in danger of paying more than the maximum, why not defer Class I contributions on one of the employments to avoid making an overpayment (see page 24)?

- Investments in:

  (i)   Pensions.

  (ii) Enterprise Investment Scheme.

        You can invest up to £150,000 in an Enterprise Investment Scheme (EIS) and you will get Income Tax relief of 20 per cent on that amount. When you sell you get full Capital Gains Tax relief (presently 40 per cent). There is a minimum investment of £500. The EIS replaced the Business Expansion Scheme which used to give Income Tax relief in the year of assessment.

        Half of the investment made before 5 October may be carried back to the previous Tax Year for Income Tax purposes (up to a maximum £25,000).

        You must hold your Enterprise Investment Scheme shares for at least three years or the relief will be withdrawn (five years in the case of shares issued before 6 April 2000).

        Any loss you make on the sale of the shares is available against either capital gains or income.

        You must not be connected with the company (i.e. hold over 30 per cent of the shares or be an employee) although you can become a director of the company and still qualify for EIS relief as long as you were not connected with the company before the shares were issued.

        Rollover relief: in addition to the above, if you have made a capital gain this year, and if you reinvest all that gain in the purchase of EIS shares, you can thereby defer all the CGT payable this year on that gain until you sell your EIS shares.

  (iii) Venture Capital Trust (see page 68).

For low earners

Young earners

Young people starting in employment have little scope for tax saving (usually because they have lower income), but they should not overlook the favourable Capital Gains Tax treatment available for those who purchase their main residence. Very few people have ever regretted purchasing their own residence.

Other low earners

Do not forget, if you are a low earner, whether in employment or self-employment, you may be able to avoid either Class 1 or Class 2 National Insurance contributions. Do not pay National Insurance contributions unnecessarily. See page 21.

Tax savings tips for children

Surplus after tax income transferred by parents to their children is usually non-taxable in the child's hands.

Make sure that savings accounts with building societies or banks in children's names are paying interest gross.

Capital Gains Tax (CGT) planning

- For married couples each spouse will be taxed on his or her own gains and receives a non-transferable annual exemption of £7,500.

- Do remember to maximise the benefit of your annual exemptions. To this end you could delay disposals until after 5 April next if you have already used your current exemption or, alternatively, bring forward planned disposals to before 6 April if you have not yet used your exemption, or split the disposals of some asset, such as blocks of shares, to straddle 5 April in order to obtain the benefit of two years' exemptions.

- Consider whether you can wait until after 5 April to make the sales so as to delay the tax payment by a further 12 months.

- Assets of negligible value: if you hold an asset – such as shares in a company – which has lost most of its value you may be able to claim the capital loss now against any Capital Gains Tax. Ask your tax inspector if he will allow the loss.

- Loans and guarantees: you may obtain relief for losses on loans and guarantees made to people who have used the money wholly for the purpose of their business. Relief is not available if the loss or guarantee arises through your own act or omission or where the borrower is your husband or wife.

- No capital gain or loss arises on gifts between husband and wife but the recipient takes over the other spouse's acquisition date and original value.

- Gifts to charities: because these are exempt from CGT it is often better, if you intend making a charitable donation of an asset which would realise a gain on disposal (e.g. shares), to consider donating the asset rather than the equivalent amount of cash. The charity may subsequently sell the shares and realise the gain free of tax because of its privileged status.

- Holdover relief for gifts: this is restricted to business assets, heritage property and property on which there is an immediate charge to Inheritance Tax.

- Do not always claim holdover relief – it is sometimes cheaper to pay a small amount of tax than to holdover the tax bill of some considerably greater sum to the future.

- All gifts are exempt from Stamp Duty.

- If you have assets which you expect will increase in value over a period of time consider giving them to your children now.

- Main residence: no Capital Gains Tax is payable on the disposal of your home. Taking in a lodger does not affect your main residence relief but letting the property does.

Inheritance Tax planning

- It is now possible to give away £242,000 every seven years without a charge to Inheritance Tax arising. However, there may be Capital Gains Tax on the gift, so take professional advice.

- There is of course tapering relief on gifts so that, as the years up to seven slip by, the tax bill does reduce significantly.

- It is important to remember, in planning to reduce the Inheritance Tax bill upon your death, not to give away too much unless you can genuinely afford to do so. Should you wish to make a gift of the family home and should you continue to live there, it is unlikely to work as an Inheritance Tax planning exercise unless you make an outright gift or you make a gift of cash to a child who uses that cash to buy the property, and in addition you pay a full market rent while you live in it. With no Capital Gains Tax arising on death it is sometimes better to let properties pass on death rather than before. However, this matter must be carefully weighed up before a decision is made.

- Lifetime gifts: gifts between husband and wife are exempt for Inheritance Tax planning.

- Remember, you can give away the annual Inheritance Tax-free exempt sum of £3,000 which may be doubled up, if exemption was not used in the previous year.

- Gifts of up to £250 per year to an individual are tax free.

- Gifts out of surplus income are tax free; take professional advice on this.

- Wedding gifts up to certain limits are tax free.

- Term assurance is a sensible means of protecting a gift that has been made should tax become due as a result of death within seven years.

- Always make a Will and build the necessary tax planning points into it. Discuss this with your solicitors.

- Special reliefs. Generally, business assets attract some measure of relief, as does woodland and agricultural property. Agricultural property without a right to vacant possession attracts a smaller relief.

- Trusts for younger children. This is a complicated subject and advice must be sought from your solicitor.

- Doubling up the main residence relief. It does not make good sense for you to buy a house or flat for your adult children to live in since any gain you make on its subsequent sale will be chargeable to Capital Gains Tax. Instead, consider providing your child with the necessary funds to make the purchase in their own name and you could do this by making an interest-free loan which you reduce each year by the annual £3,000 exemption.

- Incorporation of a growing business. It may be advantageous to give shares in the company to your children and/or grandchildren soon after incorporation when their value is relatively low.

Notable tax dates

See Appendix 12.

What is the difference between tax 'avoidance' and tax 'evasion'?

The short answer is that tax evasion is unlawful and tax avoidance is permissible. An example of tax evasion is deciding not to give either the Inland Revenue or Customs &

Excise details of all your sales (to pocket the cash and not tell anybody about the sales). This is fraudulent and will be heavily punished by the authorities when they discover it. Tax avoidance is taking the necessary legal measures to reduce your tax liabilities to the lowest permissible figure. For example, you may decide to invest in tax-free investments, such as ISAs rather than in an investment which produces income that is taxable. However, remember that the Inland Revenue have certain anti-avoidance provisions to prevent tax being saved as a result of certain activities. For example, inventing artificial transactions in land.

How should I deal with the Tax Office?

When we began in practice, some 30 years ago, the Inland Revenue staff were portrayed as ogres and inspectors were regarded as 'the enemy'. In fact, in our long years of practice, we have *always* found we have enjoyed good relations with Inspectors of Taxes and these bad reputations were both unkind and totally misleading.

However, our own observations apart, there is no doubt at all that in the last ten years particularly the Inland Revenue have become extremely friendly, helpful and courteous in their dealings. The arrival on the scene of the Taxpayers' Charter is evidence that the Inland Revenue are trying to be 'user friendly'.

Accordingly, our advice is that if you find you are dealing with the Inland Revenue, even if you are having difficulty making your tax payments, you will find most of the personnel extremely helpful, efficient and courteous and, in return, you are best advised to be efficient, courteous and prompt in your dealings with them.

In 1972, one of our authors had a letter published in the business section of *The Times* which read as follows:

> Sir, Mr Jenkins has trouble dealing with the inspectors of taxes via his accountant. May I suggest he discontinue to use his accountant as a mediator between him and his inspector? If he were to prepare his various financial statements, which he obviously does for himself anyhow, and submit them in his honesty to the inspector, he will receive help and guidance from a man who is more often than not very understanding and reasonable and, what is more, he won't have to pay for the service.

Should I use an accountant?

The arrival of self-assessment was, we suspect, originally intended to do away with the accountancy profession. After all, self-assessment implies that the tax laws are so simple that you can 'do it yourself'.

The reality, and we feel that the answers given in this book prove that what we are about to say is correct, is that self-assessment has added to the complications and responsibilities and our view is that anyone having to fill out a Tax Return should seriously consider using the services of an accountant. Not only is life more complicated but there are now penalties which were not in place before the arrival of self-assessment.

When using an accountant you should always:

- Ensure that the first meeting is free – so that you don't have to part with any money until you know whether you like the person or not.

- Ask him to quote for fees upfront and ask him if it is an all-inclusive service.

For far too long professional accountants and solicitors have churned out bills to their clients based on the hours worked x the hourly rate to give the bill. We believe that this approach is totally unfair to the client because the accountant never knows how big the bill is going to be. Instead we believe that quotations should be made upfront and they should be stuck to, and that the professional should take more risk than has been the case.

How should I handle tax investigations?

The Inland Revenue are very successful at collecting additional tax through their tax investigations and we can all expect an Inland Revenue enquiry into our affairs.

Self-assessment has given tax officers the power to make random tax enquiries. In effect, this means that they have more scope than ever to initiate tax investigations because you may now be investigated whether or not you have kept proper records.

Whilst no taxpayer will be exempt from a random audit (whether they are an individual or a business), if their accounting and tax records are in good order and if the self-assessed tax liabilities have been calculated accurately and paid on time, they should have little to fear.

When you receive notice that an enquiry has begun, you should respond promptly, courteously and cooperatively. We would normally suggest you seek the services of a qualified accountant.

How do I appeal against a tax demand if I think it is too high?

If you think the Inland Revenue has made a mistake in your tax calculation, then you should go along and get them to explain how they get to the figures.

If you are not satisfied with their explanation, or you think that there must be an underlying problem which needs special attention, then you should consult a professional accountant and he or she will do the necessary.

Postscript

A call for the Income Tax year to end on a more sensible date than 5 April

Year after year, successive Chancellors of the Exchequer fail to move this year-end by five days to 31 March, the year-end used for all other UK taxes. There is even a law, which says that the Government should end all tax years on 31 March and yet Chancellors have all, so far, failed to attend to this matter.

The facts of the matter are these:

- 5 April was chosen by accident; the date holds no importance at all and there is no intrinsic reason why we have to end our tax year on it. A change is perfectly possible.

- Inspectors of Taxes find 5 April an inconvenient date.

- Taxpayers find it inconvenient and muddling.

- 70 per cent of employers want it to be changed to 31 March.

- All the accounting and tax bodies want the date to be changed.

- Businessmen find it difficult for a host of reasons.

- The people who write computer programs for PAYE say that it would be easier for all concerned if the Income Tax Year ended on 31 March *and* it would be very easy for them to change from the present cumbersome system.

- The people who write our tax laws say that to draft the changes to the law to effect this simple change would be no trouble at all.

- The Treasury would even make money in the year of change, but not enough for us to notice paying the extra for this one year.

- Other countries have changed their Tax Years, some by more three months and have experienced no difficulty in changing.

The only reason why this absurd anomaly has not been rectified is the idleness of the civil servants who, over many years, have failed to serve their Ministers by getting on with this matter.

If you agree with me that it is absurd and ridiculous, not to say embarrassing, for our country to have a tax year that ends on 5 April, please write to the Chancellor of the Exchequer. Tell him to get his civil servants to put this change into effect and that failure to do so is not an option.

If you do this in sufficient numbers, next Budget Day we may hear of a measure being announced that will be welcomed by everyone.

Hugh Williams, FCA
April 2001

Appendices

Appendix 1 Tax rates and allowances at a glance

In 2000/01, the following rates, etc. apply

Income Tax		Taxable Income		
	Band	From	to	Rate
	1,520	0	1,520	10%
	26,880	1,521	28,400	22%
	over	28,400		40%

Capital Gains Tax (for individuals)	First	7,200	exempt
	Balance taxed at 20% and/or 40%		
	Taper relief for long-term gains. This is now complicated – consult an accountant for details.		

Corporation Tax	Band	From	to	Rate
	10,000	0	10,000	10%
	40,000	10,001	50,000	22.5%
	250,000	50,001	300,000	20%
	1,200,000	300,001	1,500,000	32.5%
	over	1,500,001		30%

Inheritance Tax (on death)	Band	From	to	Rate
	234,000	0	234,000	0%
	over	234,000		40%

Personal Allowances		
Personal		4,385
Personal (aged 65 to 74)		5,790
Married Couples (65 to 74)*#		5,185
Personal over 75		6,050
Married Couples over 75*#		5,255
All four higher age allowances are only available for incomes up to £17,000 in 2000/01		
* = relief restricted to 10% # = husband or wife must be born before 6th April 1935		

National Insurance

Class 1 (Employment)		
Employee (not contracted out)		
Earnings per week		
Up to £76		Nil
£76 to £535		10%
Over £535		£45.90
Employer (not contracted out)		
Up to £84		Nil
Over £84		12.2%

Class 2 (Self-Employment)	(The old weekly stamp)	£2.00
	No contributions due if profits below £3,825	

Class 4 (Self-Employment)	7% on profits between		
		£4,385	and	£27,820
			Maximum due	£1,640.45

State Pension		week	year
	Single	67.50	£3,510.00
	Married	107.90	£5,610.80
	over 80	0.25	£13.00

VAT		
Threshold		£52,000
Rate		17.5%
Cash Accounting Level		£350,000

Quarterly Scale Charge for Motoring		Engine Size	
		to 1400cc	1401–2000	over 2000
	Petrol	38.12	48.40	71.19
	Diesel	34.55	34.55	43.93

Taxable Car Benefits	Fuel Benefit	Engine Size	
		to 1400cc	1400–2000	over 2000
	Petrol	1,700	2,170	3,200
	Diesel	2,170	2,170	3,200

Car Benefit	Age at end of Tax Year	
	Less than 4 yrs old	over 4 yrs old
	% of price when new	

Business Miles		
Under 2,500	35%	26.25%
2,501 to 17,999	25%	18.75%
over 18,000	15%	11.25%
Vans	£500	£350

Car Mileage Allowance	Engine Size			
	up to 1,000cc	1,001 to 1,500cc	1,501 to 2,000	over 2,000cc
Up to 4,000 miles pa	28p	35p	45p	63p
Over 4,000 miles pa	17p	20p	25p	36p

In 2001/02, the following rates apply

		Taxable Income		
Income Tax	Band	From	to	Rate
	1,880	0	1,880	10%
	27,520	1,881	29,400	22%
	over	29,400		40%

Capital Gains Tax	First	7,500	exempt
(for individuals)	Balance taxed at 20% and/or 40%		
	Taper relief for long-term gains. This is now complicated – consult an accountant for details.		

Corporation Tax	Band	From	to	Rate
	10,000	0	10,000	10%
	40,000	10,001	50,000	22.5%
	250,000	50,001	300,000	20%
	1,200,000	300,001	1,500,000	32.5%
	over	1,500,001		30%

Inheritance Tax	Band	From	to	Rate
(on death)	242,000	0	242,000	0%
	over	242,000		40%

Personal Allowances	Personal	4,535
	Children's Tax Credit*	5,200
	Personal (aged 65 to 74)	5,990
	Married Couples (65 to 74)*#	5,365
	Personal over 75	6,260
	Married Couples over 75*#	5,435
	All four higher age allowances are only available for incomes up to £17,600 for 2001/02	
	* = relief restricted to 10% # = husband or wife must be born before 6th April 1935	

National Insurance		
Class 1 (Employment)	Employee (not contracted out)	
	Earnings per week	
	Up to £87	Nil
	£87 to £575	10%
	Over £575	£48.80
	Employer (not contracted out)	
	Up to £87	Nil
	Over £87	11.9%
Class 2 (Self-Employment)	(The old weekly stamp)	£2.00
	No contributions due if profits below £3,955	

Class 4 (Self-Employment)	7% on profits between		
		£4,535	and	£29,900
			Maximum due	£1,775.55

State Pension		week	year
	Single	72.50	£3,770.00
	Married	115.90	£6,026.80
	over 80	0.25	£13.00

VAT	Threshold	£54,000
	Rate	17.5%
	Cash Accounting Level	£600,000

			Engine Size	
Quarterly Scale Charge		to 1400cc	1401–2000	over 2000
for Motoring	Petrol	36.04	45.72	67.46
	Diesel	33.51	33.51	42.59

Taxable Car Benefits	Fuel Benefit		Engine Size	
		to 1400cc	1400–2000	over 2000
	Petrol	1,930	2,460	3,620
	Diesel	2,460	2,460	3,620

	Car Benefit		Age at end of Tax Year	
		Less than 4 yrs old		over 4 yrs old
			% of price when new	
	Business Miles			
	Under 2,500	35%		26.25%
	2,501 to 17,999	25%		18.75%
	over 18,000	15%		11.25%
	Vans	£500		£350

Car Mileage Allowance			Engine Size	
		Up to 1,500cc	1,501 to 2,000	over 2,000cc
Up to 4,000 miles pa		40p	45p	63p
Over 4,000 miles pa		25p	25p	36p

Appendix 2 Checklist of what to keep for your Tax Return

For Income Tax

If you receive...	Keep your...
☐ Salary/wages	Payslips (supplied by your employer) P60 (annual statement of earnings from your employer) Notice of coding (issued by the Inland Revenue)
☐ Benefits in kind *(e.g. company car, medical insurance)*	P11d (annual statement of benefits) and expense payments from your employer
☐ State benefits *(e.g. unemployment benefit, invalid care allowance, etc.)*	· Statements of payments to you by Benefits Agency
☐ Pensions *State pension, other pensions*	Statement of pension payments by Benefits Agency or Pension funds, etc.
☐ Share options *(offered by some employers)*	Share option documents from your employer
☐ Other earnings *Tips, commissions and other earnings*	Relevant vouchers
☐ Expenses not reimbursed by your employer	Expense receipts
☐ Self-employment and partnerships *Income from self-employment*	Self-employed or partnership accounts
☐ Savings and deposit accounts Banks Building Societies National Savings	Bank interest certificates Building Society interest certificates National Savings interest details
☐ Share holdings Dividends Unit Trusts	Dividend vouchers Unit Trust vouchers
☐ Other sources Annuities Other	Annuity vouchers Relevant vouchers
☐ Land and property Holiday accommodation Furnished lettings (including Rent-a-room) Wayleaves (e.g. electricity poles)	Copy invoices or receipts for rental income, etc. Receipts or supporting evidence of expenditure

If you receive income from...	Keep your...
☐ Overseas	Foreign income documents *(i.e. dividends, pensions & interest)* Foreign property income
☐ Trusts and settlements	Trust tax vouchers (R185), issued by trustees
☐ Other sources such as: Alimony Royalties Bonds, etc.	Alimony details Royalty income and expenses Bonds (called 'chargeable events'), etc.

Deductions to claim against Income Tax

☐ A loan	Loan interest statements
☐ Venture Capital Trust shares	Venture Capital Trust certificates
☐ Enterprise Investment Scheme subscriptions	Enterprise Investment Scheme certificates
☐ Charitable covenants	Deeds of covenant
☐ Gift Aid	Gift Aid details
☐ Death benefits to trade union or friendly society	Death benefit papers
☐ Or if you are registered blind	Relevant papers

For Capital Gains Tax

☐ Shares	Contract notes from your stockbroker
☐ Land and property	Estate agents particulars Completion statements (from solicitors)
☐ Paintings or other works of art	Auction advice slips Sales catalogues
☐ Businesses or parts of them	Completion statements from professional advisers

Appendix 3 Example payslip showing you how gross and net pay are set out

WAGES/SALARY PAYSLIP

Wages/salary for
Wages/months Nos:
To:

Employee's address		Week Nos.	Month Nos.	Hours	Days	Nights	@ Rate	£	p
Name									
Employer									

- P60 only
- Of Gross Pay
  £ _____ was paid by former employer.
  Of Tax paid
  £ _____ was deducted by former employer.

Gross pay

Less:
  Tax
  N.I.
  Other

£   p

Total deductions

NET PAY

	Total	Employee	Employer's cont. out
	£	£	£
	£	£	£
	£	£	£
	£	£	£

Pension details

	Employee £ p	Employer £ p	Total £ p
This period			
Totals BF	£	£	£
Totals CF	£	£	£

Income tax calculation:

Code No:

	£
Gross pay BF + this gross pay	£
Total gross CF	£
Less tax free	£
Taxable pay	£
Tax payable	£
Less previous tax payable	£

National Insurance calculation:

Gross pay for
  Week No. = £
  Week No. = £
  Week No. = £
  Week No. = £
  Month No. = £

Code
Letter:

Deductions/contributions as above

+ TOTALS BF   £

TOTALS CF   £

Appendix 4 Inland Revenue Form P11D
Expenses and Benefits 2000/01

Inland Revenue

P11D EXPENSES AND BENEFITS 2000-2001

Note to employer
Complete this return for a director, or an employee who earned at a rate of £8,500 a year or more during the year 6 April 2000 to 5 April 2001. Do not include expenses and benefits covered by a dispensation or PAYE settlement agreement. Read the P11D Guide and booklet 480, Chapter 24, before you complete the form. Send the completed P11D and form P11D(b) to the Inland Revenue office by 6 July 2001. You must give a copy of this information to the director or employee by the same date. The term employee is used to cover both directors and employees throughout the rest of this form.

Note to employee
Youer employer has filled in this form. Keep it in a safe place as you may not be able to get a duplicate. You will need it for your tax records and to complete your 2000-2001 Tax Return if you get one. Your tax code may need to be adjusted to take account of the information given on this P11D. The box numbers on this P11D have the same numbering as the Employment Pages of the Tax Return, for example, 1.12. Include the total figures in the corresponding box on the Tax Return, unless you think some other figure is more appropriate.

Employer's details
Employer's name

PAYE tax reference

Employer's details
Employer's name

If a director tick here ▶

Works number/department

National Insurance number

From 6 April 2000 employers pay Class 1A National Insurance contributions on more benefits. These are shown in boxes which are brown and have a **1A** indicator

A Assets transferred (cars, property, goods or other assets)

Description of asset

Cost/Market value £ – Amount made good or from which tax deducted £ = Cash equivalent **1.12** £ **1A**

B Payments made on behalf of employee

Description of payment **1.12** £

Tax on notional payments not borne by employee within 30 days of receipt of each notional payment **1.12** £

C Vouchers or credit cards

Value of vouchers and payments made using credit cards or tokens

Gross amount £ – Amount made good or from which tax deducted £ = Cash equivalent **1.13** £

D Living accommodation

Cash equivalent of accommodation provided for employee, or his/her family or household

Cash equivalent **1.14** £ **1A**

E Mileage allowance

Car and mileage allowances paid for employee's car

Gross amount £ – Amount made good or from which tax deducted £ = Taxable payment **1.15** £

F Cars and car fuel *If more than two cars were made available, either at the same time or in succession, please give details on a separate sheet*

	Car 1	Car 2
Make and Model		
Date first registered	/ /	/ /
Dates car was available	From / / to / /	From / / to / /
Business mileage used in calculation	2,499 or less ☐ 2,500 to 17,999 ☐ 18,000 or more ☐	2,499 or less ☐ 2,500 to 17,999 ☐ 18,000 or more ☐
Tick only one box for each car. If the car was not available for part of the year, the business mileage limits are reduced proportionately.		
Enter engine size and tick type of fuel only if there is a car fuel scale charge	Engine size in cc cc Petrol ☐ Diesel ☐	Engine size in cc cc Petrol ☐ Diesel ☐
List price of car *If there is no list price, or if it is a classic car, employers see booklet 480; employees see leaflet IR133*	£	£
Price of optional accessories fitted when car was first made available to the employee	£	£
Price of accessories added after the car was first made available to the employee	£	£
Capital contributions (maximum £5,000) the employee made towards the cost of car or accessories	£	£
Amount paid by employee for private use of the car	£	£
Cash equivalent of each car	£	£
Total cash equivalent of all cars available in 2000–2001		**1.16** £ **1A**
Cash equivalent of fuel for each car	£	£
Total cash equivalent of fuel for all cars available in 2000–2001		**1.17** £ **1A**

P11D(2001) Reproduced by Law Pack Publishing with the permission of the Controller of HMSO

RDH1132

129

G Vans

Cash equivalent of all vans made available for private use | 1.18 | £ | 1A

H Interest-free and low interest loans
If the total amount outstanding on all loans does not exceed £5,000 at any time in the year, there is no need for details in this section.

	Loan 1	Loan 2
Number of joint borrowers *(if applicable)*		
Amount outstanding at 5 April 2000 or at date loan was made if later	£	£
Amount outstanding at 5 April 2001 or at date loan was discharged if earlier	£	£
Maximum amount outstanding at any time in the year	£	£
Total amount of interest paid by the borrower in 2000-2001 – enter "NIL" if none was paid	£	£
Date loan was made in 2000-2001 if applicable	£	£
Date loan was discharged in 2000-2001 if applicable	/ /	/ /
Cash equivalent of loans after deducting any interest paid by the borrower	1.19 £ 1A	1.19 £ 1A

I Private medical treatment or insurance

	Cost to you	Amount made good or from which tax deducted	Cash equivalent
Private medical treatment or insurance	£	– £	= 1.21 £ 1A

J Qualifying relocation expenses payments and benefits
Non-qualifying benefits and expenses go in N and O below

Excess over £8,000 of all qualifying relocation expenses payments and benefits for each move | 1.22 | £ | 1A

K Services supplied

	Cost to you	Amount made good or from which tax deducted	Cash equivalent
Services supplied to the employee	£	– £	= 1.22 £ 1A

L Assets placed at the employee's disposal

	Annual value plus expenses incurred	Amount made good or from which tax deducted	Cash equivalent
Description of asset	£	– £	= 1.22 £ 1A

M Shares

Tick the box if during the year there have been share-related benefits for the employee | ☐

N Other items (including subscriptions and professional fees)

	Cost to you	Amount made good or from which tax deducted	Cash equivalent
Description of other items	£	– £	= 1.22 £ 1A
Description of other items	£	– £	= 1.22 £

	Tax paid
Income tax paid but not deducted from director's remuneration	1.22

O Expenses payments made to, or on behalf of, the employee

	Cost to you	Amount made good or from which tax deducted	Taxable payment
Travelling and subsistence payments	£	– £	= 1.23 £
Entertainment *(trading organisations read P11D Guide and then enter a tick or a cross as appropriate here)* ☐	£	– £	= 1.23 £
General expenses allowances for business travel	£	– £	= 1.23 £
Payments for use of home telephone	£	– £	= 1.23 £
Non-qualifying relocation expenses *(those not shown in section J)*	£	– £	= 1.23 £
Description of other expenses	£	– £	= 1.23 £

Appendix 5 A template to help you prepare your figures for the self-employed part of the Tax Return

Your name _____ Accounting year end _____

Self-employment and Partnerships

Sales income

less			A
	Costs of sales e.g. raw materials and stocks		
	Construction industry subcontractors' costs		
	Other direct costs e.g. packing and despatch		
	Total cost of sales		B
	Gross profit or loss A – B		C
	Other income		D

Expenditure

Employee costs
Salaries, wages, bonuses, employer's NIC, pension contributions, casual wages, canteen costs, recruitment agency fees, subcontractors (unless shown above) and other wages costs

Premises costs
Rent, ground rent, rates, water, refuse, light and heat, property insurance, security and use of home

Repairs
Repair of property, replacements, renewals, maintenance

General administrative expenses
Telephone, fax, mobile telephone, stationery, photocopying, printing, postage, courier and computer costs, subscriptions, insurance

Motoring expenses
Petrol, servicing, licence, repairs, motor insurance, hire and leasing, car parking, RAC/AA membership

Travel and subsistence
Rail, air, bus, etc., travel, taxis, subsistence and hotel costs

Entertainment
Staff entertaining (e.g. Christmas party), customer gifts up to £50 per person advertising your business

Advertising and promotion
Advertising, promotion, mailshots, free samples, brochures, newsletters, trade shows, etc.

Legal and professional costs
Accountancy, legal, architects, surveyors, stocktakers' fees, indemnity insurance

Bad debts (if already included in A above)

Interest
on bank loans, overdraft and other loans

Other finance charges
Bank charges, HP interest, credit card charges, leasing not already included

Depreciation and losses on sale (please ask for advice)

Other items – please describe

Grand total of expenses   E

Net profit (or loss) C + D – E

Appendix 6 Gift Aid declaration

Name of Charity:

Details of Donor:

Title _____ Forename(s) _____

Surname _____

Address _____

_____

_____

_____ Postcode _____

I want the charity to treat

      * the enclosed donation of £ _____

      * the donation(s) of £ _____ which I made on _____ / _____ / _____

      * all donations I make from the date of this declaration until I notify you otherwise

      * all donations I have made since 6 April 2000, and all donations I make from the date of this declaration until I notify you otherwise

as Gift Aid donations.

delete as appropriate

Notes
1. You can cancel this declaration at any time by notifying the charity.
2. You must pay an amount of Income Tax and/or Capital Gains Tax at least equal to the tax that the charity reclaims on your donations in the Tax Year (currently 28p for each £1 you give).
3. If in the future your circumstances change and you no longer pay tax on your income and capital gains equal to the tax that the charity reclaims, you can cancel your declaration (see note 1).
4. If you pay at the higher rate you can claim further tax relief in your Self-Assessment Tax Return.
5. If you are unsure of whether your donations qualify for Gift Aid tax relief, ask the charity. Or ask your local Tax Office for leaflet IR113 *Gift Aid*.

Appendix 7 A template to help you prepare your figures for the land and property income part of the Tax Return

Your name _____

Land and Property Income (year to 5 April   )

Income   Received from   Rents received
                                                                          £
_____
_____
_____

                                           Total income   £ _____

                    Tax already deducted from property income   £

                                                          £   £

Expenditure   **Premises** Rents _____
                                                     Rates _____
                                         Property insurance _____
                                            Light and heat _____
                                                  Cleaning _____
                                                  Security _____
                                                           Subtotal   [   ]

               Repairs and maintenance Repairs and renewals _____
                                              Redecorating _____
                                               Small tools _____
                                                           Subtotal   [   ]

        Finance charges and interest on loan to buy rented property   [   ]

                  Legal and professional Legal _____
                                              Accountancy _____
                                           Debt collection _____
                                           Other insurances _____
                                             Subscriptions _____
                                            Architects' fees _____
                                                           Subtotal   [   ]

                       Services provided Wages _____
                                                 Telephone _____
                                                       TV _____
                                                   Garden _____
                                                    Roads _____
                                                           Subtotal   [   ]

                             Other costs Advertising _____
                                               Agents' fees _____
                                               Office costs _____
                                                   Travel _____
                                                           Subtotal   [   ]

                                            Total expenditure   [£   ]

Appendix 8 A rough guide to Capital Gains Tax and Inheritance Tax

The effect of a .... of following items on	Gift – CGT	Gift – IHT	Sale – CGT	Sale – IHT	Death – CGT	Death – IHT
Own residence	None	Normally none, but donee must retain assets for seven years and donor must survive seven years.	None	None	None	Taxable – see note 3
Business assets:						
Land used in business	Taxable		Taxable	None	None	There should be 100% relief.
Goodwill	Taxable		Taxable	None	None	
Furnished lettings	Taxable		Taxable	None	None	
Partnerships	Taxable		Taxable	None	None	
Other assets	Taxable		Taxable	None	None	
Milk, etc. quotas	Taxable		Taxable	None	None	
Woodlands	Not taxable†		Not taxable†	None	None	See note 4
Shares in small business	Taxable		Taxable	None	None	
Let property subject to:						
Gladstone vs. Bowers tenancies	Taxable – see note 1	Tapering relief* after three years	Taxable – see note 1	None	None	Should be 100% relief
Residential tenancies	Taxable – see note 2		Taxable – see note 2	None	None	Taxable – see note 3
Farm business tenancies	Taxable – see note 1		Taxable – see note 1	None	None	Should be 100% relief
Other business tenancies	Taxable – see note 1		Taxable – see note 1	None	None	Should be 50% relief
Heritage properties	Normally taxable – see note 5		Normally taxable	None	None	Not taxable
Works of art	Taxable – see note 2		Taxable – see note 2	None	None	Taxable – see note 3
Loans to a business	Should be no CGT		Should be no CGT	None	None	Taxable – see note 3
Stock Exchange investments	Taxable – see note 2		Taxable – see note 2	None	None	Taxable – see note 3
Lloyds investments	Taxable – see note 1		Taxable – see note 1	None	None	Should be 100% relief
Trusts (interest in possession)	Not applicable	N/A	Not applicable	N/A	None	Taxable – see note 3

*Tapering relief tax charge: Death within 3 years – 100%; death within 3–4 years – 80%; death within 4–5 years – 60%; death within 5–6 years – 40%; death within 6–7 years – 20%; death after 7 years – 0%

†Standing or felled trees do not attract CGT but the land itself is subject to it

> This is only a rough guide; professional advice MUST be sought before taking action

Notes

Note 1 Disposals of business assets are subject to a number of CGT reliefs but seek professional advice, because this is only a brief summary:

Retirement relief – See main body of text.

Taper relief – See main body of text.

EIS/VCT deferral relief – an investment in shares in an unquoted trading company defers the gain. The acquisition cost is reduced by the gain.

Rollover relief – Where the disposal of business assets leads to replacement business assets being acquired, the gain on disposal is not charged to tax but the cost of the new assets is reduced by the gain.

CGT annual exemption – £7,500.

Indexation – this reduces the gain by the inflation element up to 5.4.1998.

Note 2 The following are ways in which CGT may be reduced or legally avoided:

Taper relief – See main body of text.

Indexation – this reduces the gain by the inflation element up to 5.4.1998.

EIS/VCT deferral relief – an investment in shares in an unquoted trading company defers the gain. The acquisition cost is reduced by the gain.

CGT annual exemption – £7,500.

Business losses – trading losses may be set against capital gains of that year or of the previous year, but only if they have first been set against the individual's general income for that year. They must be set off in this order, against (1) general income in that year; (2) capital gains in that year; (3) general income of previous year; (4) capital gains of previous year. Capital gains can only be offset in previous year if the business has been carried out in the previous year.

Enterprise Investment Schemes (EIS) and Venture Capital Trust relief (VCT) – an annual investment of up to £150,000 (EIS) and £100,000 (VCT) secures Income Tax relief of 20 per cent and full Capital Gains Tax relief of 40 per cent.

Note 3

Assets passing on death normally attract Inheritance Tax at 40 per cent, but the first £242,000 is tax free. Also transfers to spouses of the deceased are normally exempt.

Note 4

Property used in a business which is owned by a partner or property used in a business which is controlled by the shareholder attracts only 50 per cent relief. The property must have been used and owned for two years. Shares giving control in an agricultural company attract 100 per cent relief. Shares in a private company giving more than 25 per cent control attract 100 per cent relief, smaller share holdings attract 50 per cent.

Note 5

There may be holdover relief available.

> **This is only a rough guide; professional advice MUST be sought before taking action**

Residence and tax issues explained
What income, etc., do you pay tax on?

If you are:	Rent arising		Salary arising		Pension arising		Interest arising		Dividends arising		Self employment income		Capital Gains*		Inheritance Tax on assets	
	in UK	Outside UK	in UK	Outside UK	in UK	Outside UK	in UK	Outside UK	in UK	Outside UK	in UK	Outside UK	in UK	Outside UK	in UK	Outside UK
Resident and ordinarily resident	UK Taxable	UK Taxable	UK Taxable	UK Taxable	UK Taxable	UK Taxable up to 90%	UK Taxable	UK Taxable	UK Taxable	UK Taxable	UK Taxable	UK Taxable	UK Taxable	UK Taxable	Depends on Domicile	Depends on Domicile
Resident but not ordinarily resident	UK Taxable	UK Taxable if received in UK	UK Taxable	UK Taxable if received in UK	UK Taxable	UK Taxable as to 90% if received in UK	UK Taxable	UK Taxable if received in UK	UK Taxable	UK Taxable if received in UK	UK Taxable	UK Taxable if received in UK	UK Taxable	UK Taxable	Depends on Domicile	Depends on Domicile
Not resident	UK Taxable	Not Taxable	UK Taxable	Not Taxable	UK Taxable	Not Taxable	UK Taxable	Not Taxable	UK Taxable	Not Taxable	UK Taxable	Not Taxable	UK Tax free	UK Tax free	Depends on Domicile	Depends on Domicile
UK Domiciled	Depends on Residence	Depends on Residence	Depends on Residence	Depends on Residence	Depends on Residence	Depends on Residence	Depends on Residence	Depends on Residence	Depends on Residence	Depends on Residence	Depends on Residence	Depends on Residence	Depends on Residence	Depends on Residence	UK Taxable	UK Taxable
Not UK domiciled	Depends on Residence	Depends on Residence	Depends on Residence	Depends on Residence	Depends on Residence	Depends on Residence	Depends on Residence	Depends on Residence	Depends on Residence	Depends on Residence	Depends on Residence	Depends on Residence	Depends on Residence	Depends on Residence	UK Taxable	UK Tax free

In principle – but please take advice because this area is a minefield – the following notes should be helpful:

- Most people living in UK will be 'resident' and 'ordinarily resident' and 'UK Domiciled'.
- People born in the UK will be UK domiciled unless they change it.
- You normally have to leave the UK for one complete tax year to be non-resident for Income Tax and for five complete tax years to be non-resident for Capital Gains Tax.
- Visitors to the UK, who spend more than six months here, will probably be treated as resident but not ordinarily resident.

* Take advice on CGT issues before becoming non-UK-resident to save CGT.

Appendix 10 A template to help you work out your IHT bill and plan to make a Will

I own:	Estimated value	At my death I would like to leave this to:
House		
Valuables		
Shares		
Cash		
Other land and property		
Trust		
Business assets		
The residue of my estate		
Legacies I would like to give		Details:
Substantial gifts I have made in the last seven years		Gifted to:
Less Sums I owe	( )	How will these be repaid on death?
Total estate		
Less tax-free band	(£242,000)	
Total net		
Tax due @ 40%		

Appendix 11 Personal fact sheet

If you were to die today, how would your family and executors find your papers, etc., and sort everything out? This Personal fact sheet is a way of helping you and your survivors.

You might like to fill this in, to keep a copy yourself and place a copy with your Will.

A   **Full name** (including title and decorations)

Date of birth _____ Place of birth _____

Tax reference no. _____

State pension no. _____

NI No. _____

Others _____

_____

_____

_____

_____

This Personal fact sheet prepared (date) _____

B   **My Will**

Made on _____

Reviewed on _____

Is kept at _____

_____

_____

_____

My executors are _____ Tel no. _____

_____ Tel no. _____

_____ Tel no. _____

_____ Tel no. _____

C Substantial gifts made before death

Date of gift	Date	Value

D Location of other key documents

Funeral wishes

Keys to safe

Birth certificate

Marriage certificate

Insurance policies

Pension policies

Property and mortgage deeds

Bank statements

Building Society passbooks

Medical card

Car documents

Share certificates

Other investment certificates

Where to find brief biographical details for any obituary
(suggest who else might be able to write this)

Trust deeds

Leases of rented property

Partnership deed (copy)

E   People to contact

Accountant (see back page)

Solicitor

Stockbroker

Insurance broker

Bankers

Pension payer

Tax Office

Employer

Doctor

Trustees

Life assurance

Any other key adviser

F   My business affairs

Details

Directorships

Partnerships

G   My insurance policies

On my death the following policies mature   Location

H Employment history

From   To   Employer   Address

I My pension arrangements

Pensions payable by

Tel no.

Annuities I receive

J Other assets

Details of other assets not already listed

K Liabilities

Debts I owe   Loans

Overdrafts

HP debts

Mortgages

Guarantees I have made to

on behalf of   for £

L Clubs and organisations I belong to

M Who else has a copy of this form?

Appendix 12 Notable tax dates

Date	Significance of date	Employers	Individual Tax Payers	Partners and Sole Traders
19/4/2001	Deadline for settling 2000/01 PAYE and NIC – interest will be charged from this date on overdue balances	✓		
19/5/2001	Deadline date for Payroll Year-End Return – penalty of £100 per month for each 50 employees for any late P35	✓		
31/5/2001	Deadline date for getting P60 forms to employees	✓		
6/7/2001	Deadline date for sending P11D forms to employees and the Inland Revenue	✓		
19/7/2001	Deadline date for submission of Class 1A (National Insurance on benefits) return and payment to the Inland Revenue	✓	✓	✓
31/7/2001	Second instalments of Income Tax and Class 4 National Insurance re 2000/01 are due		✓	✓
	Another £100 fine for late submission of 1999/2000 Tax Return. A 5% surcharge where tax due for 1999/2000 still outstanding.		✓	✓
30/9/2001	Deadline for submission of 2000/01 Tax Return for tax calculation by the Inland Revenue.		✓	✓
31/1/2002	Deadline for submission of 2000/01 Tax Return. Late filers will be charged a £100 fine (and in the case of a late partnership return each partner will be fined £100) and interest on overdue tax		✓	✓
	Balance of tax due for 2000/01		✓	✓
	First Payment on account for 2001/02 tax year		✓	✓
28/2/2002	A 5% surcharge where tax due for 2000/01 still outstanding		✓	✓

Date	Significance of date	Employers	Individual Tax Payers	Partners and Sole Traders
5/4/2002	End of 2001/02 tax year	✓	✓	✓
19/4/2002	Deadline for settling 2001/02 PAYE and NIC – interest will be charged from this date on overdue balances	✓		
19/5/2002	Deadline date for Payroll Year-End Return – penalty of £100 per month for each 50 employees for any late P35	✓		
31/5/2002	Deadline date for getting P60 forms to employees	✓		
6/7/2002	Deadline date for sending P11D forms to employees and the Inland Revenue	✓		
19/7/2002	Deadline date for submission of Class 1A (National Insurance on benefits) return and payment to the Inland Revenue	✓	✓	✓
31/7/2002	Second instalments of Income Tax and Class 4 National Insurance re 2001/02 are due		✓	✓
	Another £100 fine for late submission of 2000/01 Tax Return. A 5% surcharge where tax due for 2000/01 still outstanding.		✓	✓
30/9/2002	Deadline for submission of 2001/02 Tax Return for tax calculation by the Inland Revenue.		✓	✓
31/1/2003	Deadline for submission of 2001/02 Tax Return. Late filers will be charged a £100 fine (and in the case of a late partnership return each partner will be fined £100) and interest on overdue tax		✓	✓
	Balance of tax due for 2001/02		✓	✓
	First payment on account for 2002/03 Tax Year		✓	✓
28/2/2003	A 5% surcharge where tax due for 2001/02 still outstanding	✓	✓	

Glossary

Agricultural property relief – This only relates to Inheritance Tax. Either a 50 per cent or 100 per cent reduction in the value of the agricultural land in the United Kingdom, Channel Isles or Isle of Man can be applied when listing the asset values for probate or valuing lifetime gifts.

AIM (Alternative Investment Market) – This is a Stock Exchange market whereby investors can deal in shares in unquoted companies. It was previously called the Unlisted Securities Market.

Alimony – Money payable to a former spouse after divorce.

Annuity – An annual payment to an individual, usually resulting from a capital investment. The regular annual sums cease on death. Because the payment consists mainly of a return of capital only a small part of the annuity usually bears tax at the basic rate.

AVCs (Additional voluntary contributions) – These are additional contributions by an employee to his employer's approved pension scheme or to a separate pension provider of the employee's choosing (free-standing AVC).

Bare trusts – A bare trust is one in which the beneficiary has an absolute entitlement to the income and the capital at any time.

Basic rate tax – Income Tax at 22 per cent.

Bed & breakfasting – Until the Spring Budget in 1998 it was common practice to take advantage of the annual tax free Capital Gains Tax exemption by selling sufficient numbers of shares on one day (to realise a modest tax free gain) only to buy them back the following day at more or less the same price. The 1998 Budget made bed & breakfasting ineffective for tax purposes.

Beneficial loans – This is a loan by an employer to an employee at less than the commercial rate of interest.

Benefits in kind – Otherwise known as 'perks' received by a director or an employee which are nearly always taxed as employment income.

Blind person's allowance – An allowance of £1,450 which registered blind people can claim.

Bonds – These are investments provided by insurance companies with apparently favourable tax treatment on both annual payment and final maturity. The annual payments and maturities are called 'chargeable events' by the taxman.

Business Expansion Scheme – A government scheme whereby investors could invest in smaller companies and receive tax relief in return. It ended on 31 December 1993. This scheme was replaced on 1 January 1994 by the Enterprise Investment Scheme.

Capital allowances – These allowances are given to businesses for the purchase of capital assets (usually industrial buildings, plant, machinery and motor vehicles) whereby the cost of the assets can be written down against tax over a period of years.

Capital Gains Tax – This is a tax on either the sale or gift of an asset, charging to tax the difference between the original cost and the value (sale proceeds) at disposal. If you make any capital gains as an individual the first £7,500 gain are exempt from Capital Gains Tax.

Chargeable event – *See* **Bonds**.

Class 1A NIC – These are special National Insurance contributions payable by employers on employees' benefits.

Corporation Tax – This is a tax levied on profits of limited companies.

Covenants – A payment under a deed of covenant in favour of a charity will normally benefit the charity in that the basic rate tax paid by the individual can usually be reclaimed by the charity, thereby adding to its income.

Director – A director is someone appointed by the shareholders to run a limited company. Sometimes people who are not called directors, nor formally appointed as such, by virtue of the activities they undertake in running the business, take on the same responsibilities and liabilities that a formal director attracts. Directors have certain extra responsibilities under the tax law, particularly having to report on the taxable benefits they receive or lack of them.

Discretionary trust – This is a type of trust whereby the trustees are given discretion as to the way in which they distribute income and capital to the various potential beneficiaries. In the case of other (non-discretionary) trusts the trustees are bound to pay the income over to the named beneficiaries.

Dividends – A dividend is a cash sum paid out of profits to shareholders of a company based on the number of shares they hold.

Domicile – Professional advice should be sought over this but someone who has a foreign domicile does not regard the United Kingdom as his real home.

Earned income – This is the income of an individual which is derived from their physical, personal or mental labours. It also includes most pensions.

Emoluments – This is a formal name given to salary, remuneration, bonuses and other income deriving from an employment of a director or employee.

Endowment – This usually is a form of life insurance involving payment by the insurer of a sum on a specified date, or on death.

Endowment mortgage – Is a mortgage linked to an endowment insurance policy with the mortgage being repaid from the sum insured.

Enterprise Investment Scheme – This is a scheme under which individuals receive favourable Income Tax and Capital Gains Tax treatment when investing in qualifying unquoted trading companies. This scheme replaced the Business Expansion Scheme on 1 January 1994.

Filing date – 31 January, being the date following the end of the Tax Year by which your Self-Assessment Tax Return must have been submitted to the Inland Revenue if you are to avoid an automatic £100 penalty.

Free-Standing AVCs – *See* **AVCs**.

Fringe benefits – *See* **Benefits in kind**.

General Commissioners – Ordinary people who hear tax appeals and decide either in favour of the taxpayer or the Tax Inspector.

Gift aid – Whereas deeds of covenant must be written to last at least four years, gift aid covers individual single donations to charities from which, so long as basic rate tax has been deducted, the charity is entitled to reclaim the tax. A form has to be obtained from the Inland Revenue, filled in and handed to the charity.

Golden handshake – Term given to a lump sum payment made by an employer to an employee on the cessation of their employment. This can usually attract favourable tax treatment.

Gross income – Income from which no tax is deducted at source, even though tax may still have to be paid.

Higher paid employee – Anyone paid over the surprisingly small sum of £8,500 (including taxable benefits).

Higher rate tax – Income Tax at 40 per cent.

Holdover relief – This is tax relief given to a donor, or other transferor of business assets whereby the gain is not charged to tax but deducted from the cost of the asset in the hands of the recipient.

Income Tax – This was the tax introduced in 1799 to pay for the Napoleonic wars and is still with us today.

Indexation allowance – This was the deduction allowed on all taxable gains up to 5 April 1998 for the element of the gain from 31 March 1982 onwards attributable to inflation. It is not available for that part of any gain which has accrued since 5 April 1998 (except in the case of companies).

Inheritance Tax – This is the tax payable on assets transferred on death and by way of lifetime gift, although estates (including transfers in the previous seven years) do not pay tax on the first £242,000.

Inheritance Tax exemption – It is possible to give away £3,000 each year (the annual exemption) with no reporting to the tax authorities. If you did not use the previous year's exemption it is also possible to go back one year and include that as well, thereby doubling up the exemption to £6,000.

ISA (Individual Savings Account) – The new tax free savings account introduced by the Labour Government and launched on 6 April 1999.

Lodgers – *See* **Rent-a-room relief**.

Lower-paid employees – Anyone receiving less than £8,500 per year including benefits in kind.

Lower rate tax – Income tax at 10 per cent (on first £1,880 of taxable income).

Maintenance – A term for the payments made by one spouse to another after divorce.

MIRAS – The acronym for 'mortgage interest relief deducted at source'.

Mortgage – A debt secured by a document (called a mortgage deed) which gives security to the lender for the debt. The mortgage deed must be returned at the time of settlement of the debt.

National Insurance – This is a 'tax' applied to employment income and self-employment income, the contributions going towards the state pension on retirement and other contributory benefits.

Net relevant earnings – This is the total figure of earnings on which maximum entitlement to pay pension contributions is calculated. They are basically either the employment income or the self-employment income, less certain deductions.

Overlap relief – Where a self-employed business suffers tax more than once on a particular year's profits, a figure of overlap relief should be calculated so that, in due course, usually on the cessation of the business, this overpayment of tax may be taken into account.

PAYE (Pay As You Earn) – The compulsory system for employers to use whereby tax and National Insurance are deducted more or less evenly over the year resulting in the correct amount of tax and National Insurance being paid by the end of the tax year on an individual's earnings.

PEP (Personal Equity Plan) – This was a government tax-free system for investing in stocks and shares which was available up until 5 April 1999.

Potentially exempt transfer – A gift made by an individual that, so long as the donor lives for a further seven years, will not attract Inheritance Tax.

Private residence relief – This is the relief that exempts any gain on the sale of the home of an individual from Capital Gains Tax.

Relevant earnings – *See* **Net relevant earnings**.

Rent-a-room relief – Special relief for individuals who let rooms to lodgers in their homes.

Retirement relief – This is a relief against Capital Gains Tax for self-employed and partners who dispose or sell their business. It is being phased out.

Rollover relief – This is a Capital Gains Tax relief that is available to an individual or partnership or a company which disposes of one business asset and uses the proceeds to acquire a replacement business asset during a specified qualifying period.

Schedule A – Income from land and property is generally assessed under Schedule A.

Schedule D – Business profits are assessed under Schedule D.

Schedule E – Directors and employees are assessed under Schedule E.

Schedule F – Dividends are assessed under Schedule F.

Self-employed – Someone who is working in business on his own, preparing accounts and paying his own tax and National Insurance contributions. Note: It is often a moot point as to whether somebody is self-employed or employed and professional advice should be sought.

Settlement – *See* **Trust**.

Share options – This is an option granted to employees (usually) whereby they may buy shares in the company for which they work.

Stamp Duty – This is the duty payable on transfers of shares and properties.

Taper relief – The new method (since 5 April 1998) whereby capital gains may be reduced on the basis of the number of complete years of ownership of the asset being disposed of.

Tax avoidance – Legally arranging your affairs in such a way as to reduce your tax liability.

Tax evasion – Illegally avoiding a tax liability – evade tax at your peril!

Term assurance – This is a cheap form of life assurance whereby, on the death of an individual within a certain specified time, a capital sum will be paid. This can be useful for providing for possible Inheritance Tax liabilities.

TESSAs – Tax Exempt Special Savings Accounts. New accounts can no longer be opened after 5 April 1999.

Trust (otherwise known as settlement) – Property is held in trust where the owner has passed it to trustees who hold it and manage it under the terms of the legal deed called the Trust Deed for the benefit of the beneficiaries.

Unearned income – Income from investments as opposed to income earned.

Unincorporated business – Partnerships and sole traders are unincorporated businesses. Limited companies are incorporated businesses.

Unit trusts – An investment fund investing the combined contributions from individual investors and paying them dividends in proportion to their holdings.

Venture Capital Trusts – This is a type of investment trust for investing in unquoted trading companies with significant tax advantages for the investor.

Wasting assets – This is an asset that has an anticipated useful life of less than 50 years.

Wayleaves – The land and property income deriving from sundry items such as telegraph and electricity poles.

Widow's bereavement allowance – For two years after her husband died, a widow was entitled to an allowance called the 'widow's bereavement allowance'. This allowance was abolished with effect from 2000/01.

Will – Legal document that shows how a deceased person wished his estate to be distributed, and who was to administer that estate. For further information on Wills consult Law Pack's *Last Will & Testament Guide*.

Index

This index covers all chapters, but not
appendices or Glossary. Terms refer to taxation,
the principal subject of the book.

A

accountants 26, 119-20
accumulation and maintenance settlements 83
additional voluntary contributions, free-standing
    44
Advance Corporation Tax 90
agricultural buildings allowances 54
allowances 13, 91 *see also* expenses; reliefs
    agricultural buildings allowances 54
    capital 54
    children's 15
    industrial buildings allowances 54
    married couple's, limitations 14
    non-residents 96
annuities 45
purchased life 67, 71
appeals, against demands 120
assets, trading, disposal of 79
associated companies 88
audit trail 104
authors 56
averaging, farm revenue 55

B

B & B (bed & breakfasting) 63
banks, interest payments 66
bed & breakfasting (B & B) 63
benefits
    allowances see allowances
    for employees 36-8, 112-14
        National Insurance on 40
    for employers 112, 113
    expenses 33-4, 49-52 *see also* allowances;
        reliefs
    travel, dispensation 38
    vehicles 36-8
    or low earners 116

for personal taxpayers 114-15
    reliefs see reliefs
    self-employment 114
    for young adults 116
bonds 70
building societies, interest payments 66-7

C

capital allowances 54
capital assets, losses 77
Capital Gains Tax (CGT) 34, 49
    complications 74-5, 76-7
    and Corporation Tax 91
    dates 116
        payment 78
    disposal element 75
    exemptions 74, 76
        non-residence 97
    vs. Income Tax, property deals 64
    indexation 76
    liabilities 74, 75
        chattels 79
        disposal of trading assets 79
        gifts 79
        homes
            as private residences 78
            working from 49, 78
        land 78
        limitations 76
        non-residents 80
        part-disposals 78
        partnerships 59
    limitations, retirement relief 79-80
    planning 116-17
    taper relief 75, 76-7
    trusts 83
Capital Transfer Tax *see* Inheritance Tax (IHT)
cars
    car scale charges 36-7
    Fixed Profit Car Scheme 37-8
casual employment 30
categories 2-3 *see also* individual tax categories

More books from Law Pack....to order call 020 7940 7000...

Cohabitation Rights

As more couples choose not to marry, the legal and financial issues they face with children, mortgages, separation and death become ever more important to understand and address. This book includes the options in cohabitation agreements and living together agreements and provides practical advice for couples.

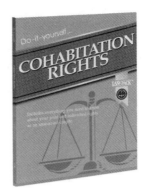

Code B423	ISBN 1 902646 52 5	PB
246 x 189mm	88 pp	£9.99	1st edition

Residential Lettings

This Guide is required reading for anyone letting residential property. It provides all that a would-be landlord needs to know before letting a flat or house. It covers the legal background, preparation of the property, finding a tenant, the tenancy agreement, problem tenants, buy-to-let, HMOs and more.

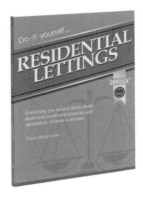

Code B422	ISBN 1 902646 51 7	PB
246 x 189mm	120 pp	£9.99	1st edition

Small Claims

If you want to take action to recover a debt, resolve a contract dispute or make a personal injury claim, you can file your own small claim without a solicitor. This Guide includes clear instructions and advice on how to handle your own case and enforce judgment.

Code B406	ISBN 1 902646 04 5	PB
A4	96 pp	£9.99	2nd edition

More books from Law Pack....to order call 020 7940 7000...

Probate

What happens when someone dies, with or without leaving a Will, and their estate needs to be dealt with? Probate is the process whereby the deceased's executors apply for authority to handle the deceased's assets. This Guide provides the information and instructions needed to obtain a grant of probate, or grant of letters of administration, and administer an estate without the expense of a solicitor.

Code B409	ISBN 1 902646 27 4	PB
246 x 189mm	96 pp	£9.99	2nd edition

Powers of Attorney & Living Will

You never know when you might need someone to act on your behalf with full legal authority. What if you became seriously ill and needed business and personal interests looked after? This Law Pack Guide explains the difference between an Enduring Power of Attorney and a General Power of Attorney and shows how to create both. With the Living Will in this Guide, you can also express your wishes regarding future medical treatment.

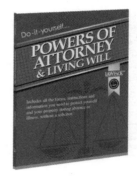

Code B410	ISBN 1 902646 69 X	PB
246 x 189mm	104 pp	£9.99	3rd edition

Employment Law

Whether you are an employer or an employee, you have rights in the workplace. This best-selling Guide is a comprehensive source of knowledge on hiring, wages, employment contracts, termination, discrimination and other important issues. It puts at your fingertips all the important legal points employers and employees should know.

Code B408	ISBN 1 902646 61 4	PB
246 x 189mm	148 pp	£9.99	4th edition

No. 2
BESTSELL